Let Go and Let Love:
Survivors of Suicide Loss
Healing Handbook

Let Go and Let Love: Survivors of Suicide Loss Healing Handbook

Gabrielle Doucet

Let Go and Let Love: Survivor of Suicide Loss Healing Handbook
By Gabrielle Doucet

www.survivorhealing.com

Printed by CreateSpace, a DBA of On-Demand Publishing, LLC
4900 Lacross Rd. North Charleston, SC 29406
(843) 760-8000 www.createspace.com

ISBN: 1512190098
ISBN-13: 9781512190090
Library of Congress Control Number: 2015907801
CreateSpace Independent Publishing Platform
North Charleston, South Carolina

Printed in the United States of America

Cover design by Scott Bricher. Assisted by Julie O'Donnell. Edited by
Lisa Fugard

Dedication

This book is dedicated to all mothers who have lost
their beloved children, wherever and whoever they are.
We all share the loss together.
We are One.

"It's not the knowledge that you finished the task perfectly. It's the fact you were called to do it in the first place, and then did the very best you could."

—M.L.F.

Table of Contents

Some Words About Drew · · · · · · · · · · · · xi

Introduction · · · · · · · · · · · · · · · · · · 1

Chapter 1   How to Use This Book and the Tools · · · 11

Chapter 2   Intention ·20

Chapter 3   Deep Breathing· · · · · · · · · · · · · · · · · 51

Chapter 4   Gratitude and Appreciation · · · · · · · · ·83

Chapter 5   Part I - Silence and Meditation · · · · · · 108

Part II - Release · · · · · · · · · · · · · · · 129

Chapter 6   Allowing and Zero Judgment · · · · · · · 143

Chapter 7   You Manifest What You Think · · · · · · · 171

Chapter 8   The Now Moment: Be In It And
Experience It · · · · · · · · · · · · · · · · · 195

Chapter 9   The Long Haul · · · · · · · · · · · · · · · ·225

Acknowledgments · · · · · · · · · · · · · · ·253

Resources and References · · · · · · · · · ·255

About the Author · · · · · · · · · · · · · · ·263

Some Words About Drew

"And when no hope was left in sight
On that starry, starry night
You took your life as lovers often do
But I could have told you Vincent
This world was never meant for one as
beautiful as you...."

— DON MCLEAN – 1971

SPEAKING AS A MOTHER, WE all believe our children are special, in some way or many ways. Drew was exceptional, even perfect to many. He wasn't of course, we all know that. Looking back though, there were times when Drew appeared to embrace the ideal life. As a child, he never wasted words; he developed an honor and loyalty to others that was evident but never spoken about. Lean and tall like his grandfather, handsome in a way that Hollywood would appreciate, and super intelligent to the point he could accomplish anything he ever wanted. And it was well understood that the party didn't start until Drew arrived.

Being the first child he was the cowcatcher for all things learned, both good and bad, and never failed to share the secrets with his sister and his friends. Never with his parents. I had to find out where all the bodies were buried at 2 a.m. on a Christmas-Morning-Post-Christmas-Eve party that wouldn't quit. There we all were in the wee hours of the morning, consuming the last dregs of our wine, Drew and his closest friends, and us, his parents all sitting around. The fire in the grate was nearly ash when the stories began. First little innocent confessions, then the really big admissions about the fire in the woods that brought the fire department creating a sink-hole in the front yard, the hockey puck depressions in the downstairs recreation room walls, the missing lamppost. Drew was over twenty-one by this time and I have to admit it was a true eye- opener to find the truths of these things, years later after blaming half of the neighborhood during his growing years. When I am with his best friends we still laugh until tears roll down our faces about the revelations. Every once in a while more stories emerge and I am still amazed at what we as parents never knew.

Drew was devoted to his sister, five years his junior, though Emma was not quite sure of this in her younger years. Typical of families, a baby sister becomes an object in the way of a big brother's playtime, so she was basically tolerated until she earned some years. That was when Emma and Drew discovered they truly had so much in common. The most obvious was their sense of humor and intelligence—a most dangerous combination for and towards everyone else. They harbored a special bond that no one else in the family could really compete with. I knew in my heart that a majority of the time they could communicate with each other and never say a word.

When Drew moved away from home, initially for his college education, and then when he secured a position in his educational field, it became apparent that he was maturing in different ways. When we first deposited him at the university way out of state, he didn't know a single person. He called home every night asking to come home. He said he had made a terrible mistake and had never been so unhappy. By Christmas, I did not recognize the mature and confident young man in front of me; he belonged to a fraternity and had made friends that would last his lifetime. Drew's friends remain devoted to his family to this day, and I know these loving, gifted people have enriched all of our lives. They are valued beyond measure.

Like all adults moving on in their lives, his personality shifted to accommodate a new lifestyle. He had chosen to enter a stressful profession, so I was not surprised when some impact of that appeared on his face from time to time. Other things came, too; a wife, a new home, a mortgage, children, money issues—the things of life. Were there changes? Yes, subtle ones. Could I interpret them as more than that? No. Some sort of OCD was making headway in his daily behavior, but that isn't deadly, is it? It's just that there was more going on beneath his demeanor that we were unaware of and would never know about until much later. Drew continued to be a man who didn't give anything away of his emotional situation, of that he was the perfect con man. The lines deepened on his face, a change in the eyes perhaps, and according to his wife, his anxieties pulled his brows together even during sleep. I suspect we will never understand exactly where it all changed for Drew.

In the spring of 2011, my son took his own life at forty-one years of age. We never saw it coming. After the immediate storm of his death had passed, his family, like everyone else, had so many questions. Were we to assume that his legacy was merely to co-create beautiful children, gather life-long friends and make a huge contribution to his chosen profession and then vanish from the earth's census? Or was it something greater than that? Is there something greater than that? For me and for many people like me, there is always something greater.

For those readers who may look to the spiritual realm, as I do, I wish to tell you about an experience I had regarding Drew following his death. As a nurse, I am primarily a person of science, but since 2003, nearly a decade before Drew's passing, I have found, as no doubt you have, that there are occurrences that go beyond the explainable. We all feel them from time to time; coincidences that defy the norm. Over the years I simply accepted them as they came. This instance is just one of those occurrences.

This event came just four days after he ended his life. At this point we were driving each morning to his home to try and make some sense out of the chaos and wait for the officials to give us permission to complete arrangements. As I drove the fifty minutes in my truck, I was about two-thirds of the way to his house when a large white figure appeared beyond my windshield and hovered over the pavement in front of me, keeping pace with the truck's forward movement. The shape was deep and wedge-like, not dissimilar to what a wine-stopper might be—all broad in the shoulders and coming to an angled point at the base. Above the flat shoulder-wedge was something of an oval. I put my complete focus on this image and had no thought about who would drive the truck. That swift lack of concern was itself remarkable. I never gave it a second thought. I truly was dumb-struck at what was before me and how it was unfolding. I knew it was Drew. He allowed me a few minutes to get some bearings and then said—in my head—"I am completely at peace. Do you see there are no lines on my face? My face is smooth." His countenance was not something I could describe then or now, but my feeling was that Drew was gently resting and hovering without any effort. He said nothing more, just stayed weightless in front of the vehicle and me. It was pleasant being in his presence, like old friends standing together. I am unable to acknowledge the total time this took to have this experience, but after it ended I had passed at least two exits on the way to his house and have no recollection of driving the truck. How can this be? I lost time, but we never deviated from the road or even our lane. My dear friend, who was riding shotgun, had no idea what was happening next to him. The vehicle never varied from the road in any way. It was 11:15 am. Earlier, I had called a colleague of mine and asked her to please email our circle of friends and let them know what had happened in our life. She decided to do this communication at 11:15 am on the same day and time I was driving the truck. At that moment, Drew appeared to her in a similar white image and asked her to see how clear and peaceful his face was. Two days later she conveyed this information to me and I was stunned. She saw almost exactly what I saw – neither of us had an explanation for it. This first encounter was a shock, but not at all frightening. Rather, it was comforting and eased some of the pain in my heart.

I cannot explain how and why this appearance took place, as well as several others I will reveal in this book, but they were clearly real for me. As scientific as I am, I have chosen to be open to the unusual and the mysterious. It is my belief that if we close ourselves down from grief, fear of the unknown and the unexplained, we lose the chance to be a connection between one plane and the next, one world and another. I will not see Drew in the flesh in this lifetime, but I will embrace the possibility that I might be able to reach out to him in another energy form and find solace.

I cherish the before and the afters. They are much of what fills that deep hole within my heart. The good thing about all of the memories is that I do not, will not, bury them along with my son. The beauty of owning them is that I can bring them out whenever I want to and show them to whomever I please. You will learn to do this, even if you can't right now. The outcome of capturing and sharing your memories will bring joy to you and everyone else.

Introduction

"Sometimes a moment arrives when you are so
unprepared for what follows that your mind just
sort of stops. Everything you know with certainty
is simply washed right out of your brain; a sort of
paralysis, if you will. It is replaced by messages
so incomprehensible, that it requires herculean
strength just to move your eyes. Suicide—the loss of
someone we love by their own hand. At the moment
of impact it becomes crystal clear that we are not
going to survive this. We can't even say the word."

—M.L.F.

*Suicide. It's here; it's now a part of my life and it is irrevocable.
I stand completely in the dark. There appears to be no roadmap,
no headlamp for finding my way into any kind of light again.*

I don't have any choices; they have all been made without me. What are my options? Yet, somewhere deep in my soul I begin to believe there are actually some decisions I can make if I look hard enough, if I am determined enough. Somehow, I heard myself saying to me, "I cannot be totally without tools to get me through this, right? Drew may now be out of options, but I refuse to be!"

Now, as I recall that morning in Spring 2011 when I awoke to a panicked phone call from my daughter-in-law, only to end the day with the surety that I would never see, touch, embrace or talk with my son ever again in this lifetime, it is hard to imagine the journey between then and today. And yet, I managed to negotiate that pathway to now without crumbling under the weight of it. I found the way to keep from endlessly trying to comprehend the why of losing Drew to suicide, and instead I managed *my* life in response to it. That still small voice in my soul told me that I did, and still do, have choices that I can make that meet my needs and move me forward every single day. Tools of survival existed that helped keep me from the crumbling. Tools I still use today—years after Drew's passing. I am stronger now than I ever was before.

I wrote this book as much for myself and my own healing as I did for you, the reader. If you are reading this, it is most likely because you have lost someone who chose suicide to exit this world. Or possibly you may be someone who is researching suicide, and for whatever reason, it is important for you to understand the complex healing process that we the survivors must go through. I read somewhere the statistic that for every person who is a victim of suicide, there are no less than eight closely related and family related survivors who will deal with the immediate and long-lasting fallout. It is my experience that the number may be too conservative – I honestly believe it could be closer to ten. And if it accurately spirals up into the double digits, then we have a lot of agony and healing to manage, especially with a topic no one wants to talk about.

This book may have its origins in the suicidal act, but it proposes methods for doing something for the better, rather than waiting for something better to happen. Perhaps it will not be from an angle you have considered up until now, because it is not about graphs and spreadsheets, statistics, and exhaustive lists of contributing mental illnesses. Above all, absolutely no descriptions of ground zero. For this author, the tragedy has occurred, and how it was carried out was a matter for the medical examiner. This book is all about helping people to go forward; speaking directly to the families, friends and acquaintances of the victim and what they can do to get their hearts, minds and lives on track again. Throughout these pages, I will give you tools that you can learn to use, that will put you in charge of your own journey and good health. You will be in possession of the incredible gift of influence over your emotional environment, when you want it. You will carry it with you at all times. All you need to do is pull out the tool required from your internal learning station and put it directly into play at the very moment you need it. What an opportunity we have before us, just when we thought all of our choices had been taken away. As survivors, we will never forget, we will never be the same, but we can face life with surety, and we can find joy.

The definition of a survivor of suicide is not an individual who is attempting to end their life by their own hand and is somehow stopped or saved from doing so. A survivor of suicide is one who is left behind after a loved one completes the act. The most recent terminology used for describing us is "survivors of suicide loss". It is a mother, father, sister, brother, son, daughter, family member, friend, colleague, or neighbor. In other words, it's all the rest of us.

Being a survivor of suicide loss is a lifetime journey from here on, so let's get fully prepared to make that journey count.

Our society indicates, both verbally and non-verbally, that suicide is a taboo discussion for the living: if you are touched by it, every conversation about your loved one's death is most likely tainted with how the majority of the world sees it. Thus, the word "committed" is added to suicide as if this is a crime—worthy of an investigation from the police department and the legal system. And indeed, suicides almost always do involve law enforcement, by virtue of the fact civil servants must make sure that there was no foul play connected with carrying it out. Alas, another stigma we as survivors must endure in the precious moments and hours after learning our loved ones have been lost to us. *No one outside this situation can possibly comprehend the stunning blows we are experiencing at this time of grief.*

It has taken me a while to formulate the following images into words, but I have decided that each suicide, the effects of which spiral outward into the unknown, gigantic depths of society, essentially creates three initial rings around the victim. This response would be similar to the rings that move outward from a central point of contact within a body of water. The touch point is the loss, and the circular expansion outward is the reaction and response to that loss.

THE RING OF FIRE

Within this group are those people whose lives are forever and irrevocably changed. These would be the immediate family and people that are considered family. According to statistics, there are approximately 8 to 10 people in this circle. In general, the people forming the Ring of Fire are, at the onset, permanently scarred, temporarily paralyzed and totally lost without a safe mental foundation, and this can last for a very long time. The first ring survivor's existence each day is living in the shadow of someone deeply loved and lost, not from an accident or illness, but by free will. In the Ring of Fire there reigns confusion, anguish and desperate isolation. The other two rings will probably never fully comprehend what those in the first ring are experiencing—total consumption through chaos. There is nothing to be done.

THE RING OF QUAKE

For ring two, the ground has totally shifted beneath them and they cannot get their footing. What they thought they knew and believed has crumbled and they don't know where to go from here. These might be close, social, even lifelong friends, next door neighbors, college mates, cousins, associates such as military/police/fire, and perhaps the siblings and parents of these same second ring individuals. It is hard to say how many folks find themselves in the Ring of Quake, but it is going to be decidedly more than in the Ring of Fire. The Ring of Quake wants to help everyone in the Ring of Fire, but honestly do not know how because they are in their own painful spot. They do the very best they can, but there is an unspoken effort to escape being too close to the inner ring for too long.

THE RING OF IMPACT

Here you might find co-workers, neighbors, gym-mates, athletic coaches, physicians, counselors, and others dependent on some type of connection, information and/ or work from the victim. It's not that they are just sad and shaken, but their daily or weekly life might be impacted by something the victim supplied in some way— even if it was a visit or luncheon engagement. Their lives have changed and they need to rethink a lot of what they had always accepted as a given. The Ring of Impact people can feel very sad but they have little idea how to convey this well to others.

As you read this book you will intuitively know which ring you fall into, but know that you may find yourself in more than one ring. It is all part of the process as it unfolds and it is inevitable. Each ring has its own set of needs and it is the other rings that are most likely going to contribute to those needs in some way.

So why this book? Why now? I know in my heart that we, as survivors of suicide, have the opportunity through our loss to be a bridge between the victim and the rest of society. Since they can no longer speak for themselves, it could be up to us to help our communities and the world to better understand a victim who feels so trapped in their own pain that personal problem solving is beyond their reach and escape is the only answer. Even with a final note the victim may have written, survivors do not really have any acceptable clues as to the reasons their loved one devalued their lives so irrevocably. Honestly, does a rational, clear mind come to the conclusion that suicide is the only way to be free? Given the opportunity, the people lost to us would have much to say in the wake of their passing that would help us clarify motives and outcomes, but since that is no longer possible, it can be the rest of us who can speak out and speak freely about a subject that remains hidden and misunderstood. Let's embrace that as a major step to our own healing.

So what we are left with is going forward, or not. We can provide a context that is a celebration to their life while still respecting their right to end it...or not.

It is not just about surviving the death of someone we love by suicide; it is truly about thriving in the aftermath of it. If you are reading this and you are convinced that you cannot possibly embrace life again after suicide of someone close to you, I am here to tell you that you can. I am not just the author here; I am a "thriver" of all of the physical pain, black holes, anguished and guilt-ridden endless days and totally sleepless nights that can accompany the life of anyone who is left behind.

I will candidly tell you of my fears and emotions on the day of discovery. The reason for that will be for you to safely identify that what you experienced, and are perhaps still experiencing, has been familiar to countless others like you and before you. From here on in, we learn and BE in the moment and we love and move forward.

In the last couple of years, I have made some very conscious decisions about my life as it will be and my son's life as it was. To that end, I believe that there are many wonderful and dedicated people who are providing support and counsel to mentally anguished survivors surrounding death in any form. We need those groups and counselors who assist us to comprehend our emotional environment, share our experience, contemplate next steps, and to play an active part in getting on with life. However, there also seems to be an enormous shadow space that accompanies us when we are "out there" on our own. How to deal with those moments is what I am looking to address. I am speaking about the motivation we must have to welcome in the day – and the next day and the next. I refer to the intention we create to live a bountiful, joyful life while still remembering and holding our loved one dear and close in our hearts throughout our life. What philosophy is out there to help us with that? The only action required is to love. Love yourself and love the person you have lost and do it unconditionally. But love yourself first!

I feel the need to include a useful and quotable resource base without bringing a whole cadre of scientific data and references here. If I quote information that will enhance understanding, I will do so only to prove or illustrate a point. I don't want to impress you on research. I want you to have tools you can use to live life every single day. Tools, I have and tools I will share.

That is the story I want to share with you—how I regained my footing, my laughter, my appreciation and my joy. This is my story after losing my son Drew to suicide and it becomes my legacy to you. I hope with all my heart that it helps you find life wonderful. We are looking for hope. We want to embrace life again because we are alive and we seek a bright future for ourselves every time we rise from our beds and greet the day.

I do. And so will you.

CHAPTER 1

How to Use This Book and the Tools

"There is a community of the spirit. Join it, and
feel the delight of walking in the noisy street and
being the noise. Drink all your passion, and be a
disgrace. Close both eyes to see with the other eye."

—Rumi

As a Registered Nurse for several decades, and a person of Spirit, I have spent my last eleven years working with people on how to improve their health and reduce stress through the mind-body connection. Early in my nursing career there was very little implementing done in this realm; medicine was focused on the science of the body, not the "feelings" of the body. I believe, know and practice differently now that I understand that through education, mindfulness and adjustment of environment, we can gain a more balanced lifestyle. In this professional role, I design space that moves us away from the stressors of everyday life that we all face and into better health. It is all about our energy, how we use it and where we direct it.

Several years ago I developed a program in which my clients could experience personal healing from a variety of conditions: pain, injury, fear, anxiety, sadness and chronic/acute illness. This program put them in control and gave them tools to work with so they could function minute to minute, on their own—out there. It allowed them to eliminate the feeling of helplessness and being completely at the mercy of daily life and whatever their health condition presented. The point is my clients could leave the confines of the training session and use the knowledge they had gained after they went out the door.

You do not need to imagine the personal test I faced when suicide of a family member entered my life. Either the rubber of my current belief and teaching was going to hit the road and propel me forward, or my body would forever stay immobile on the pavement. I not only faced the torrential onslaught of what suicide brings in its wake, but I now needed to apply my skills to the severest stressor a human, in my opinion, can encounter.

In the spring of 2011, I had to put my actions into play or curl up in a terrible ball from which I might never emerge. It became a deal-breaker in my life.

I want you to know that this book is for you. It has been written just for you, and for survivors of suicide loss, just like us, all across this planet. To that end, why not make it work for you as a reference, a journal, a hope, a friend, a discussion tool, a pocket guide or a heart and hand warmer? Nothing can be more personal than suicide, and your situation is not going to be like anyone else's. All we do is think, think, think about this; so as you encounter the topics and guidance in here, why not capture your questions and issues as they occur? Further down the line in another chapter, another page, another sentence, the answers may come. Just in case the answers don't surface for you, let's talk about it. I am completely available to assist you through this journey, so contact me and we will chat about your situation and how to apply it to the tools here. You will find my contact information in the resource section at the close of the book.

Allow me to briefly list here the tools with a short description for each, just to get you oriented for what is to come. As I have mentioned earlier, the tools appear in the order that I have felt makes the most sense; but you make the judgment for yourself how they work best for you. They are virtually unchanged from how I first introduced them to my clients, the exception being that I would sometimes shift the tools of Gratitude, Silence, Allowing, Manifesting and The Now Moment, depending on the needs of the client with whom I was working. When dealing with suicide loss, the tools require different examples, methods of application and interpretations to enhance understanding. Whatever the healing need, these are tools for life. We will discover unlimited opportunities for using them in any situations we find ourselves.

1. *Intention:* This is a simple statement that captures in words what you would like to have, become, achieve or be. A positive desire that you are working on and have not yet worked out. It involves your thoughts, emotional input and mind-set.

2. *Deep Breathing:* Breathing deeply, you allow your body to receive the stressor, decrease the physical reaction to it, and the brain tissues get the oxygen and nutrition to help you get through to the other side of it. Know and understand what constitutes deep breathing, and become familiar with the simple steps of the activity.

3. *Gratitude, Appreciation and Abundance:* Being grateful is 180 degrees away from anger or negativity. Look at your emotional responses to any situation that is painful, and find the opportunity for change.

4. *Silence, Meditation and Release:* Interrupt Doing and embrace Being. Provide our minds and bodies a chance to have a voice – from the inside out. Learn the methods for letting go of what no longer serves us.

5. *Allowing and No Judgment:* Recognizing, through deliberate action and understanding, everyone's given right to have a thought, opinion or personal declaration that works just for them with no explanation to anyone else.

6. *You manifest what you think:* What you are primarily thinking and saying in words is what you will manifest and receive. This is also known as the law of attraction.

7. *The Now Moment:* We recognize the emotion or feelings we have, and we are looking at them as they are occurring in our life at this very minute. By observing them, we are accepting their existence without responding or using a judgment.

You will notice that every time we move to a new tool, I try to find a way of defining what the tool is and why we are using it. It may sound rather academic, but often we miss the real words that are used in defining what we know. Words are important, especially so in this text. If what we think is what we manifest, and I base my entire belief system on that premise, the tool defined is the tool in action. If healing is the desire, then the action we take toward healing needs to be clearly understood.

The tools that follow are in an order that make sense for learning and engaging progressively. I feel the most critical are listed first, but let me just say that they can be moved around according to your situation and personal needs. The first two tools, Intention and Deep Breathing, need to be highest on the list of what to think about first. They seldom move out of those positions, so try to keep that in mind if you are one to skip sections and move around.

Another factor that should be helpful in this process is that many of the challenges survivors face every day are often grounded successfully in the use of more than one tool. Much later in the book we will explore how the combinations of tools can work together and successfully assist you through the more complex challenges and, ultimately, the healing. First, you need to learn and engage each tool separately. I would encourage you to begin using every tool as you learn it; apply it for real even if you think it will not help you. You have absolutely nothing to lose in giving every suggestion a chance right from the start.

Each tool has its own set of solutions for you to use, as well. Within each suggestion lie some examples of what I, and others, have encountered in our path through survivorship. You may easily recognize yourself there or we may not have captured an exact situation that you have or are experiencing, but hopefully we have come close enough for you to apply it successfully.

To engage these tools and subsequent healing you need to do the homework. It takes a determination and a desire to feel better than you do right now. So if you are perhaps hoping that by just reading the words on the pages you will miraculously change, I am pretty certain that won't happen. I wish it were so. What it will require is to learn about each tool and put it to use for real. At the end of each chapter I include practices that demonstrate how you can exercise each tool and give it application in your everyday life, starting immediately.

Try to remember that if you are learning about deep breathing, but then continue to move your life-giving oxygen in a shallow manner throughout your body especially when you are stressed, deep breathing will not give you its phenomenal benefits. Soon you will learn your first tool of Intention, and when you do, the following sentence can be your very first intention practiced – "I am committed to trying these tools in the best way I can each day." Practice, Dear Reader, it is the only way that you will feel the change and the difference from what it was like prior. Don't let your first Meditation exercise throw you; you will learn to quiet your mind, but maybe not so easily the first (or second or third) time. Above all be patient with you. Be gentle on you. You are, after all, the most important person in the world, working in a very human vessel.

Finally, this is not a race. My singular caution to you is to take your time with each chapter and give it your full attention. Examine your feelings about the tool's purpose and application, both now and in the future. Try it out repeatedly before you move on to the next tool. Let's face the reality that we cannot gather up all the tools and suddenly start using them all at once. That is not practical, nor does it give you the opportunity to see how each tool works in your world. When you think you have a handle on one tool's approach and usage, and you are beginning to use it in real time—and seeing positive change!—then move on to the next tool. Give yourself time to assimilate – engage it in "out there" usage.

If you have tools of your own and they are working perfectly for you – I rejoice. I would also love to have you share with me the healing methods that are moving you through these difficult stages. Get in touch with me and let's talk about that. However, if you are reading this book, it might just be that techniques and activities are not working so well and perhaps you can consider new ways to help or augment your progress. *The goal is to bring our own survivor healing into the light.* When you leave the safety of the home, church, counseling session, group meeting, wherever, embrace the possibility that you can make a difference in your life and health for the rest of your life just by changing your perspective on how you see survivorship. You are a survivor of suicide, but that doesn't mean you have to be a victim of life. You are worthy of the best of everything.

CHAPTER 2

Intention

"The more aware of your intentions and your
experiences you become, the more you will
be able to connect the two, and the more you
will be able to create the experiences of your
life consciously. This is the development of
mastery. It is the creation of authentic power."

—GARY ZUKAV

AT SOME POINT, IN THE period of time that follows a loss,
any loss, we begin to search inwardly for answers and
guidance. This is especially true after someone close to
us has taken his or her own life. Intuitively, we understand that we need "something," and we suspect that we
should be able to name it and declare what it is, but it
is just not that easy to do. No manual is included with

suicide-loss recovery, and answers within this search seem to elude us at every turn. *What am I to do now? How will I ever understand what they did and why they did it? Who am I now? Will people ask me horrible questions and will l have to answer them?* We need a pillar of fire to give us a direction or at least set us on a course, but we are on our own here.

In my case, I looked left and saw my son's wife who was in her own terrible place with two small children to manage...and it was her job to explain what happened to their father. I looked right and saw my sweet daughter, sister to Drew—the person she most looked up to in life—and observed confusion and anger and a newborn. Who was going to help whom here? We were blind people leading blind people.

In the days that followed Drew's death, I was numb. Very little made sense; I felt pushed from location to location, bed to clothes closet, kitchen to car, table to funeral home—even my thoughts felt pushed around without any particular input from me. I was unable to visualize a destination on my own, simply because getting from point A to point B required footing of some sort, and the ground beneath my feet was pretty much gone. My ability to make decisions had been fouled. When I did problem solve, I quickly forgot the steps I used to get there; therefore, the outcome seemed mysteriously lopsided. I rapidly learned I couldn't effectively make any type of plan in the hours, days, and weeks that followed the event. During this time period I was just trying to survive this siege to the human body and mind.

I kept thinking over and over, how could it possibly be that everybody else's life is moving on? They needed to stand still, just like I was. People went back to work, meals were made, bills continued to arrive in the mail and were being paid, and babies got their diapers changed. Didn't everyone around me realize that someone really important died here and my life would never, ever be the same? The time for me to begin using the tool of intention was coming, and the need to use it would happen sooner than I imagined. But it was not here quite yet; I, like you, would need to get through the shock of the loss first, however long that took. (By now you may well have gone past the point that includes the initial numbness. But where are you right now, and are you seeing any light on a pathway out of the darker spaces?)

Then, somehow, miraculously, intuitively, I did what I have always done. I went into survival mode and I focused in on the one individual that I trusted the most. Me—the person who knows everything about Gabrielle. I grabbed on to what I believed in: the teachings I had been sending out to clients for the last year, the knowledge that we (I, You, Me) are the best resource we will ever have. I started using the teachings as if my life depended upon it. And, indeed it did; because, honestly, I needed to find a good reason to stay here! I turned to Intention.

The dictionary version of intention is simply too literal for me as a survivor: that is, setting a goal, planning steps to get from point A to point B, making lists, doing and doing and doing. I have developed a much more accurate and compassionate definition for those of us who sometimes run on the edge of helplessness and being overwhelmed. *An Intention is a simple statement that captures in words what you would like to have, become, achieve or be, in any given situation or condition that you find yourself. It surrounds a positive desire that you are working on and have not yet worked out. It involves your thoughts, emotional input and mindset, not your muscles.*

Believe me when I tell you, survivors of loss should not set intentions that require their muscles and brains – instead, the intentions should have everything to do with healing that focuses on the emotions and heart. Intentions became for me, short bursts of positivity that moved me forward in small deliberate steps. My personal intentions got me on my feet, reaching for miniscule wins and celebrations. Gary Zukav, who supplied the quote at the beginning of this tool, further states; "Your intentions are your nonphysical causes that set energy into motion…" Knowing what I know now and coming as far as I have, I could not agree more. Our intentions should stem from the non-physical. If we seek to put effective healing energy into motion, intentions will be formed and birthed in the emotional realm, not the muscular one.

Some of you reading this are probably saying to yourself, "I have tried affirmations before—this never has and probably never will work for me!"

Let me share with you what I think of as the major differences between affirmations and intentions. For me, they don't feel like they have the same dimensions. Affirmations feel bigger than intentions; they appear to incorporate a larger picture in the quest for self-guidance, but aren't necessarily our creation nor totally in sync with that which is presently happening in our lives. Can we bridge the gap between where we are and where we want to be by using an affirmation or an intention? Here are some affirmations you may have read or heard: I am successful in everything I do; I will find the perfect job; I have all the monetary abundance that I require; I am safe, I am healthy, and free of pain; I think positively at all times. Do you think any of these statements of affirmation will help you manage a crisis or situation *in the moment?* Intentions, on the other hand, can set a positive focus for an hour or a day, even for a few precious minutes. Sometimes that is all we can manage within loss.

I have used and still use affirmations in far deeper ways than the cerebral reasons for which they were created. Dr. Wayne Dyer, internationally known self-help author and motivational speaker, in his lectures for *Wishes Fulfilled*, has described affirmations as "an intellectual exercise," not generally aligned with the intense "feeling" needed behind it to spur you on to the success you desire. How I agree! Without the gut-feeling punch behind them and your committed belief, they may not do much. However, if your motivation seems to run to affirmations, that's fine, you can mentally make that phonetic substitute every time you read the word Intention. Please be cautious that your affirmation/intention doesn't run to the grand scheme, is possibly formulated by someone else who determines it is wise and good for all, and blithely projects your life out into undefined time frames. Within healing after loss, we are prudent to progress in small, incredibly clear steps. In the throes of sadness, worry and grief, intention is what I cling to. When I am praying for help in getting through one encounter, you can bet that a specific intention will be my hope for deliverance.

I prefer to ask my intention to help me move, allow me to move, intend me to move, and even more, to see myself moving through a small but powerful declaration of positive change accompanied by a ferocious emotional feeling.

Intention setting is the true groundwork for all of the tools that follow here and it can be tricky to grasp. You may think that it borders on the abstract, and perhaps it does to some degree, but as in all things important to this life, it requires you to trust in yourself above all others. When you set an intention for yourself, you will need to step right out on its limb and trust that it will not fail you. If it is going to work for you, you will state your intention and thoroughly believe in it. This is what I did; and no matter what happened or what anyone else said to me, I chose my intention and then watched it manifest for me, healing me every step of the way, even if it was only for the next hour. I was now one hour further along!

You may ask why is Intention at the very beginning of the list of tools for getting back my life after suicide? The answer is: *without having your eyes on the outcome; it will be very difficult to see the path that leads to it. It is a stepladder for climbing out of the slippery, unhealthy dark areas and getting on solid ground.*

* Every intention made, no matter how small, is another small light for your feet to move in.
* Every intention made opens a door, however slight, to a positive outcome.
* Every intention made brings about a subtle change in behavior. It may be so minute at first

that you may not notice it but your subconscious does! It listens to what you are saying and wants to bring it to you.

* Every positive outcome resulting from an intention reinforces that the journey to good health is in front of you and success is imminent. Your belief in the intention and its desired result is reassurance to your emotional guidance system.

* Every intention made is the basis for learning and engaging the other six steps that follow. Intention must be accomplished first, because it must bring with it the emotional feeling that is always your secure guidance system in action.

It doesn't matter whether your loved one left last week or seven years ago. We all progress through things differently and at our individual paces. Only you can determine where you are right now, so it is up to you when you want to begin using intention, but why not start here? Believe me when I say, *It is all about you.* If you can find relief in the heart, you will be able to better process your next step in the lighted journey.

It All Affects the Body

With any loss comes some form of physical pain. Inside of our bodies the time it takes to show up may be in slow motion, but it is coming none-the-less in some form and degree if we remain unaware. It may emerge as a general lack of good health, joints that ache, headaches, visual issues, hearing discrepancies, abdominal and elimination discomforts, sleeplessness. Physical pains ride aboard any number of vehicles, and will often manifest from robust fear, anger, and as many of us have learned, from loss. I learned that while assisting clients long before Drew died. Understanding this brings a very powerful message—*there is an intense connection between physical pain and the mental and emotional condition.*

Let me tell you about a family that I met along the way during my research. Their child, a sixteen-year-old we will call Joel, having everything in life ahead of him, ended his life just prior to a yearly celebration at the family ski house. The reasons for his decision, sadly, rest with him. It's the father that I wish to focus on right now. Here was a man completely and understandably devastated by the suicide of his only child. This tragedy descended on a closely-knit family and without warning. In the fourteen years that have passed since losing his son, he has refused to talk of anything related to the day Joel died. He has quietly removed himself of any part of a conversation that includes suicide and specifically, Joel. Within the gathering I was attending, many of the folks were aware of the book I was writing and openly engaged in talking with me about their experiences and those of people they knew. At that moment, he quietly slipped away and moved to another location completely outside of the group. His sister informed me that her brother cannot and will not give voice to his own story. She shared that over the past several years he has developed diabetes, high blood pressure, swelling of the knees, an eating disorder and severe weight gain. Now you are asking yourself; Gabrielle, how can you positively relate his current health situation to the suicide of his son, and perhaps of his own behavior following it? I can't. But as a nurse and survivor, I would probably lay some serious odds as to whether the two situations are connected. Over these many seasons, he has swallowed his anger and grief, guilt and silence—and become sick.

If we use Intention to positively adjust how we face the moment, the day, we have one powerful tool for forestalling and possibly removing the opportunity for negative *physical* response. In the case of the father in the story, I would imagine over the years there would have been hundreds of small intentions that would have given voice to his needs and comfort to his emotional condition, thus relieving his body of dangerous stressors.

Intention helps us to articulate our desire for clarity. Remember the questions we faced—"What am I to do now? How will I ever understand what they did and why they did it? Who am I now, if not their father, brother, mother, cousin?" By formulating a statement that is good for us toward answering these queries, we provide very little reason for our bodies to break down under duress. Intentions can give us a way to address getting over the mountains, by conquering the hills one at a time. *We are marvels of our existence, not mules to it.*

"There is nothing wrong with dreaming, but there is everything wrong with dreaming without any intention to make the dream a reality."

—UNARINE RAMARU

Steps to Setting an Intention

1. *Identify an issue that you see as a trigger and want to change for the positive.* An example could be something that is a recurring situation, such as fear of discussion of suicide surrounding your loved one.

2. *Verbalize your feelings around this issue and state clearly how it relates to you.* For example; if fear of opening up or participating in suicide discussions is part of your daily existence, use your emotionally charged desire to be free of fear, as well as your given right to choose the topics you wish to take part in. Use that as the basis for your Intention.

3. *Formulate the response exactly as you would like it to be*, for exactly as long as you think it should be or as long as you can manage. Use your emotions to guide you in the formation of the Intention. For example; in an effort to give zero power to fear, form an intention such as, "Today, I will state clearly and calmly that I am not ready to talk about this now, and that is good." You declare that you will not enter into the conversation, so you remove any power from fear as a possible outcome.

4. *Say exactly what you want to say, to whomever you need to say it to.* Visualize yourself saying/doing so, or find every opportunity to practice it ahead of time.

5. *See yourself moving out of an unwanted position successfully.* If you don't think you did it as perfectly as you would like, always celebrate your attempt. You will get it right. Just don't stop trying.

In the case of Joel's father, if he had formulated and used this intention, he likely would have eliminated the fear of dealing with any discussion, especially when it came up unexpectedly. Rather, he would be making a statement that would give his audience a clear understanding of his needs. In time, he could formulate another intention that moves him further along in the healing process, yet continues to create the limits he can manage. Example: "I will acknowledge Joel's name and that he took his life on (date,) to whoever asks, the very next time it is necessary."

USE INTENTIONS ON A DAILY BASIS
Especially when you are met with difficult or unexpected situations, having an intention will get you thinking in the right direction. What is it you need *today*? How is your heart feeling *today*? What will help you move forward *today*? You needn't look beyond today's challenges, tomorrow will assert itself soon enough. The following are just some of the situations you may have been experiencing. We all know that our real daily life is different from anyone else's, but somewhere in the upcoming examples you will make a connection, get the message and feel the excitement that it was exactly what you needed to hear. The scripts will follow the five steps of intention usage and will get you started in addressing the very encounters that you come against every single day. (Further along in this book we will encounter another of the steps to guide you, known as The Now Moment.) Why not be in this moment, starting right now and face some awesome healing just today?

MEDICAL AND MENTAL ISSUES OF THE DECEASED
Perhaps your loved one had been treated for various medical and mental conditions long before he or she

acted on the situation. Perhaps they were not in a long-term struggle that you were aware of or participated in, and new information following their death is coming to you now. It can make you feel blindsided. I learned information shortly before and after Drew's passing that totally baffled me, since he chose to keep everything to himself. Whether or not this is the case for you, it can be devastating to learn information in hindsight and know you can't do anything about it now.

Step 1 – Identify the Issue.
Example: I consistently think about and worry about, "What if?" I am burdened with thoughts of guilt.

What sorts of worries or anxieties confront you that set your intense emotional reaction into play? How are you experiencing it? Within this step you must state it clearly and without censorship to yourself or to someone you trust who knows you and your responses. Without censorship means to be honest; do not sugarcoat the dilemma as you face it. This is not the space to *solve* the issue, just to *understand* the issue via your own description.

Step 2 – Verbalize a statement of the issue as it relates to you and what you would like to change.
Example: *I am exhausted* with ideas that I am somehow responsible. *I do not want to think* that I missed clues or the opportunity to prevent the tragic outcome.

This is a good moment to state with surety that you couldn't have done anything about it ever. Or perhaps you spent countless hours attempting to remedy these issues for years prior to suicide; but again, this was beyond your control and in reality never was in your control. Medical documents are informative and may provide some clarification, but they are essentially useless at this point. They may create more questions than provide answers, and therefore become extremely difficult for you to process during grieving. You may learn that your loved one refused or stopped counseling, making or keeping physician visits, or ignored prescribed medications as a treatment plan. That is just the way it was in their very personal decision-making process. Their physical and/or mental condition was unacceptable to them and they were unable to see a solution to even some of the smallest of dilemmas.

Step 3 – Formulate the response exactly as you want it to be
I will believe/embrace/accept the fact my loved one was in a struggle that he or she could not get free from. I could not fix this before and I cannot fix this now. I am not created to fix anyone.

This is an intention you formulate in advance, based on your current emotional connection to undeserved guilt. It is best thought of each morning before you begin your day. Find times during your daily routine to bring it to mind in readiness for the unexpected. Practicing it whenever possible prepares you for the times you may need it the most—for your own wandering thoughts or the thoughtless statements of others. Put your emotional power of believing in yourself directly behind the intention. It is true for you now and it is true for you always.

The tendency to find guilt for yourself in their life scenario will make this intention challenging, but you can do it. You will not only repeat this intention to yourself, but to others who will want to pull you and themselves into the stream of what-ifs and should-haves. Your intention will keep you strong.

Step 4 – See yourself saying/doing it
Because you can and should spend the time saying an intention to yourself regarding guilt, you will learn to have it resting on your tongue waiting for its debut to others. Each time you say it with feeling and committed emotional input, it registers in your consciousness as truth. That is just what you need, because it is your truth. When the time comes, this intention will provide you with the support that gives guilt-free success.

Step 5 – See yourself successful in releasing guilt and fear
Example: I *see* myself breathing, free of worry and clear of mind. I will tell myself I have always done everything

the best way possible. I hand the responsibility to the one person it belongs to and send them love.

Congratulations on following through on your desire! If it didn't go perfectly, you will adjust for the next time, right? Even if you hesitated, but got it out, you have met your lighted path head-on. Thank you for being firm in stating your truth to yourself and perhaps someone else.

REACTIONS OF FAMILY AND FRIENDS

As you are probably discovering or have already learned, there are as many reactions to this suicide loss experience as there are stars in the sky. There are always those who are embarrassed and have absolutely no idea what to say, or people you hardly know who are unbelievably compassionate. Probably one of the worst responses is from people who want to know all of the details; how it happened, what they did, who found them. And this questioning is accompanied by a compassionate look and gesture, but let's just call it what it is—morbid curiosity. This has no place in your healing space!

Let me give you some examples of reactions that stunned me. The first one was from my sibling that was so unexpected and baffling that it took an Intention that I had to ground-hook onto the earth's core before

I could keep steady. My dear family member stopped talking to me completely. She wouldn't hug me, comfort me, excuse my incoherent words, forgive, understand or find kindness for me. I not only lost my son, I virtually lost my last family connection. What was I guilty of?

Clearly one of the hardest things we must do sometimes is to face cold hard reactions and behaviors from others that may not be repairable, and just seem to hurt even more. Just in case you have experienced this scenario or one similar, let me bring you right through the five points of intention forming for the challenge I faced with my sister.

Step 1 – Identify the trigger Issue

My sibling is somehow so angry with me that she will not speak to me in a civil manner, touch me or comfort me. I don't know what I have done to be on the receiving end of such painfully negative behavior. I have no idea how I can deal with this now, let alone fix it.

Step 2 – Verbalize the issue as it relates to you

I am so sad and confused about her rejection, and this is on top of the current misery of losing my son. I must not try and solve this situation; I need to conserve my energy, what little I have left.

Step 3 – Formulate the response (i.e. my "ground hook" intention)

I am committed to my healing. I will allow that her (their) beliefs, inquiries and curiosities surrounding this tragedy are inconsistent with my ability to move safely forward, so there is nothing here to remedy. I will let these exchanges/anger/questions go, and the individuals will need to take care of themselves. My process is more important than anyone else's.

This is an intention that is guaranteed to start your healing, that first determined forward step on the lighted pathway you have before you. No wishy-washy statement here – a flat out declaration of independence for you!

Step 4 – See yourself saying/doing it.

In my example of my sibling, for the next three days, I stood in front of the mirror and said (as if my sibling were in front of me), "I love you, but you are on your own. My concern is my well being for the hours and days ahead. The door is open if you should change your mind, but I have no regrets and require no explanations. I only go forward!" (The caution here is to be sure that the intention you have formulated is one that you will thoroughly believe in. This is not the time to allow doubt to generate another guilt-ridden package to your consciousness.)

Step 5 – See yourself successful in releasing worry and indecision

A great weight has been lifted off of my shoulders by accepting that others do not necessarily agree with my actions or beliefs. That is totally acceptable to me. I let all differences go without blame or recrimination. I am completely comfortable with my decisions because they are right for me.

A similar example came from several of Drew's friends who were furious with him for not coming to them for help. They ranted at the fact that what he did was, in their opinion, a cowardly act. All he had to do was open up and spill his feelings, state or somehow indicate his plan for self-harm and they would have come to his aid. They looked directly at me and said these very things. I was stunned. Do you know who you are talking to? You are saying this to his mother! My son didn't share his deepest anxieties and confusion with his own family, why in the world would he spill his guts to an acquaintance or even a close friend?

We all react to this horrific event differently and sometimes completely without appropriateness. Handled with a well-thought-out intention, it need not be permanently injurious or personally directed. Without my intention firmly in place, I would not have come through these types of encounters without damage.

In this second instance, I followed the intention-forming steps, very similar to the ones I used for my sibling. The intention I finally formulated was done in advance, because I felt certain there would be encounters in the near future that would parallel what I had already heard. I wanted to be ready for the feelings that arise in any group setting. It was as follows:

I am a survivor, but I am not responsible for the situation we now find ourselves in. I will be tolerant, if I can, of what others say and think, but I will not accept it as my thought or as truth. Their opinions will not influence what I know to be true, and that is, all victims are victims.

Effect on the Community

Group counseling for survivors of suicide is so helpful and needed because, as survivors of suicide loss we do not really fit anywhere else. We are associated with that "S" word and it does not easily come up in discussion, nor is it handled very well when it does. And when it does get brought into the open, you recognize the look on the faces of strangers and acquaintances and your saliva dries up. It's not that we are situational pariahs; it's just that suicide is scary for everybody, so as far as the general population is concerned, stay away from talking about it!

Are you having difficulty saying the word? Do you describe the loss of your loved one as someone who was "ill" and lost a fight with a deadly sickness? Do you create another scenario to avoid it all? Do you stammer and stutter when another person wants to know what happened? I remember the first time a new acquaintance asked me how many children I had. My pause was so long, it shocked even me! Simple answer for a simple question, right? I didn't know these people – they had no right to be privy to such personal experiences, and there I was with my tongue in a knot while they waited for a response. I cannot imagine what my face was reflecting. Finally, I looked them in the eyes and said, "I have two children, boy and girl, both grown." And that was that. I had made it over the hurdle, certainly the worst one of the week, and I didn't fall apart, or lie, or betray anyone. This couple didn't really qualify to know my private horror, but what should I do next time when it is with someone I know well? What will I do?

One of the best outcomes you can shoot for is to pre-think as many scenarios as possible and make a response plan. Not all of them can be anticipated, but it all boils down to how you can be most comfortable. Plan for it and then say it. At some point you will need to be up front with people in the community about how suicide has touched you, because frankly, that information is out there anyway. Until you are, know what your comfort zone will be and make your Intention. You can say the word suicide whenever and wherever you want; or not, you decide.

Step 1 – Identify the trigger issue
I am not comfortable talking about suicide. It's a very hard word and it touches me deeply. People ask simple common questions about my family and in my mind, complicated answers loom. I don't know what to say and feel cornered.

Step 2 – Verbalize my feelings
I want to stop being afraid, and instead want to be ready and comfortable to guide a discussion in the best way possible for my healing journey at this point.

Step 3 – Formulate my Intention
I am in charge of what I communicate from this moment forward. I will be honest with myself and then with whomever I speak to, but it will always be on my terms. My loved one's action will not tongue-tie me and keep me from speaking my truth. It begins now.

Step 4 – See myself saying/doing it
I am calm and collected when certain subjects arise in a group. I see myself saying such sentences as: "Thank you

for asking, but I would rather not talk about that now."
"Yes, that is true. I am doing better every day with my acceptance and understanding of the situation."

Step 5 – See myself successful in releasing fear
I did it! I said what I wanted and didn't say what I felt uncomfortable with. It all worked out perfectly.

EFFECT ON MY WELL-BEING

Even if it's *all about me* and *I am the most important person in the world,* I still feel like crap every single day I wake up and face the truth. My loved one is gone, I didn't get a chance to see them, talk with them, help them, and I feel imprisoned by my unique situation every day before my feet hit the floor. I resent the fact that other mothers have their sons to walk down the street with and hug whenever they want to. It makes me angry when I see people taking no notice of what they have right in front of them. They take it all for granted. *Try walking in my shoes, people!*

Everyone is walking in some kind of shoe—not all of them are comfortable ones either. When I felt resentful of what I saw on the street every day, I knew I had to get a handle on regrets, on envy, on jealousy of someone's family unit. My family is forever changed, but wanting that for anyone else out of spite is just not helpful for me or humane. I cannot tell you the number of times I wanted to say, "Just imagine if you lost your ..." That is a ghastly picture that can get stuck somewhere the very moment you draw it and let it pass your lips.

Is it possible you can be grateful for them? Without justifying your sadness and situation, can you for one moment bless them on their abundance and wish them well as you move along? Look at the scenario in front of you and remember how you interacted with your loved one in a joyful way. If you can do that just once, right then, you can do it again, and then again. Appreciating your loved one's time with you is glorious in hindsight and healing in this very moment.

Step 1 – Identify the Issue

* Example A: My loved one is gone. My chances to be with them ever again have vanished. I feel imprisoned by my unique situation every day and I often resent the loving interactions I observe around me. It makes me angry for what I no longer possess.
* Example B: Everywhere I look, I see myself as being sad.
* Example C: I keep myself so busy that my day is filled with tasks and obligations until day's end. If I stop moving, I break down.
* Example D: I can't bring myself to ask for help from anyone and cannot find the words to

honestly declare what will help me. I say Yes when No would be better for me.

Step 2 – Verbalize my feelings

* Example A: I don't want to be resentful—that's not who I am. I want to be happy for anyone who loves and enjoys their family and friends. It is their right to be joyful.

* Example B: I always used to smile, laugh, be spontaneous and have fun, but that has not been the case since losing my loved one. I am afraid and angry that I have lost this genuine ability.

* Example C: I worry that I am not facing my grief. I am concerned that my busyness is a way for me to avoid the depths of my sorrow and anger.

* Example D: I am exhausted with trying to figure everything out myself. I carry an enormous burden and at times I wish for trusted help in lifting it off.

Step 3 – Formulate my Intention

* Example A: I am in charge of what I think from this moment forward. Right now I will push resentment aside and embrace a wonderful memory.

* Example B: I will find one thing to genuinely smile or laugh about at least once each day this week. I will consciously remember something funny about my loved one today; then I will tell someone about it and laugh out loud. I will do something unexpected today for myself or someone else that will make us both smile.
* Example C: I will set time aside for me. I will visit a peaceful spot today where I can read my favorite book or just sit and breathe.
* Example D: I will speak my truth today about what I need—or don't need from others—and not feel guilty or selfish about it."

Step 4 – See myself saying/doing it

* Example A: I can see myself smiling when two people are holding hands and talking animatedly with each other. I see myself sending them a true blessing at that moment. I remember when I did that very same thing with my loved one. It became a wonderful memory when it happened.
* Example B: I see myself smiling. I allow myself the vision of actually laughing at anything that is funny in my conversations today. I think about what it will feel like to laugh and know it is good.

* Example C: I see myself peaceful and without a timeline related to myself or someone else. I allow myself to take these moments without guilt or the need to rush. I intend to stay here as long as I wish.
* Example D: I see myself letting go of the unnecessary whenever possible. I watch myself allowing support by trusted resources. I visualize saying no-thank-you when it is in my best interests and feel good about it.

Step 5 – See myself successful

* Example A: I am less resentful every day! I feel more happiness for others than I have been able to do before. This is so much easier than being angry – I want to continue my healthy progress.
* Example B: I am successful at finding something to smile at or be happy about more and more. I am reducing the burden of sadness each time I interact with someone and I know this is true. My mind is less heavy and my conscious thoughts are lighter!
* Example C: My calendar has openings that are clearly set aside for me and for quiet time. There is such a difference in how I feel about busyness and allowing myself to reflect on grief when I need to do so.

* Example D: I know I am successful because I am saying No when I think I should or when I am clear that it is in my best interest to do so. I have been saying Yes only when I want to say yes! What a wonderful relief.

Practice Guidelines

Formulate your Intentions every day, as many times a day as you need or can manage. Is it one per week? Good for you—there are no set rules on how many and in what time frame.

* Commit to the process of intention setting. Believe everything you say, even if it is difficult or seems impossible. It isn't impossible. If you think you are faking it, smile and tell yourself that it is temporary. You will believe it –really—next time.
* Start with an intention written in advance for a situation that you know you will need. Practice it in your head, so it is right on your tongue. Place them everywhere you want as a reminder.
* Think about other intentions, either from the examples in this handbook or ones of your own.
* Say it out loud, look in the mirror at yourself and say it, repeat it at the time you arise and before you sleep. Smile when you say it.

* Write it down and put it where you can see it and read it whenever you want. Put it on post-its at home, work, in the bathroom, near the coffee pot, on the car dashboard, where you keep the dog-leash.
* When you are feeling good about forming an intention and practicing it, do another one. Make a list; use one or ten a day or one per week. It needs to work for you, not anyone else.
* Believe your intentions with your whole heart. They are working just for you. *They are working –* period!

Have you noticed that every single one of the sample intentions began with the word "I?" That is not a mistake. *It is all about you. You are the most important person in the world. If you don't make yourself this important, you will not be able to open yourself to the rest of the world and everyone and everything in it.*

Your intention will be your starting point. If the intention you have formed doesn't hit the mark, reform it and try it again, especially if you know you will need it. If you can't accomplish it yet, that is ok, simply spend some time identifying what triggers are the ones that set you in a tailspin or tempt you to avoid routine interactions with others. That will be time well spent and before you realize, you will find the words that will give your

Intention its power for you. Please do not give up setting an intention. Try saying it out loud. Use your voice. Remember, it is your lighted pathway to the goal of a healed heart. A healed heart may never fully remove the hole left behind, but it can bring softness to its edges, and create a place for you to put good memories for safekeeping.

CHAPTER 3

Deep Breathing

"Breath is the bridge which connects life
to consciousness, which unites your body
to your thoughts. Whenever your mind
becomes scattered, use your breath as the
means to take hold of your mind again."

—THICH NHAT HANH

"You don't have to be under water to
feel like you are drowning. Take a
deep breath – it will save you."

—M.L.F.

WHAT I HAVE JUST BEEN *told, is not possible. I can't believe this
has happened. I won't believe this has happened.* At that

moment and in the moments that followed discovery of Drew's suicide, I could not breathe. Where the hell was my air? My lungs did not seem to be working! My body seemed to be in some sort of crisis and it involved my ability to take in oxygen.

If my medical background has taught me anything about our human body systems, it is that everything is designed to work together. The autonomic system and the sympathetic system – better known as "fight or flight" – are part of a magnificent machine: you and me. Most of the things that our bodies do from millisecond to millisecond, pretty much happen without our intervention. Breathing is one of the only things we participate in, both consciously and unconsciously. We can pay attention to it or not, our choice. We cannot live without our breath; our organs must have oxygen to do their individual jobs, and the brain will only operate at maximum capacity and efficiency with oxygen in our system. That's on a normal day, within normal circumstances.

Under severe duress, as I described myself in the first paragraph, we frequently restrict our air intake by hyperventilating and/or breathing shallow, sometimes holding our breath entirely. This reduces the air to all organs and primarily the brain where we need it the most – especially in a stressful encounter. This is a good opportunity to provide a definition of fight or flight and many of you will know about this. What the greatest majority of us don't know is that fight or flight (F&F) takes place in our bodies without our conscious permission. The reaction is a built-in design, no intervention required. The sympathetic nervous system in the human body is always on autopilot. As a result of a real or imagined life-threatening event, the body prepares to do one of two things; run with every muscle and bone at your disposal in the opposite direction, or put up your dukes and prepare to defend yourself. Whether you flee or stand your ground, your heart rate will greatly increase, the breathing rate does double time, tons of blood and nutrients will flood to your brain, nerves and muscles, parts of the body will sweat bullets, the hairs on your arms and head will stand straight up and adrenaline will come pouring into the bloodstream from every direction. At this point the automatic parts of this response are all in place and functioning. However, somewhere in the middle of all this action, we can begin to be consciously aware of the breathing changes we are experiencing. We can hold our breath or hyperventilate; in which case fainting is common, since neither hyperventilation nor lack of ventilation are conditions that sustain consciousness for very long. Fortunately, we are so well designed that a good faint simply restores our natural breathing rhythms and we wake back up. The best news of all really is that following the immediate F&F response, we can soon begin to consciously regulate our breathing to our benefit. The moment we cognitively register what our breath is doing, we can begin breathing in a way that will sustain our chosen action, (running or standing firm), and take control again.

What about when true fight or flight has not been biologically triggered? By that I mean, we are experiencing a stressful encounter not on the scale and level of F&F; when something else is in progress and we detect our body is responding in a way that feels scary, confrontational, but not deadly? In this situation, greater than 90 percent of us will still not breathe properly, creating an air-deprived condition, increasing peril to ourselves in another way. F&F is extremely short-term simply because your physical body cannot sustain it for long and wasn't meant to. Other stressful responses in our daily life will not engage F&F, but will trigger bodily reactions remarkably like a fight or flight. Unmanaged, these stressful outcomes can certainly do us damage in the long run. Can we do something useful about that? Can we help ourselves through a crisis just by using our breath?

Can you remember what happened to you physically when you were confronted with the news of your loved one's suicide or the moment of discovery? For me it was heart-stopping, breath-arresting and earth-shattering. The impact on my body and all of its systems at that instant seemed almost beyond measure. I can honestly postulate that I came as close to experiencing my own death at that moment as I have known. There wasn't a "deep breath" available to me for 100 miles in any direction. I was, and you probably were, in a supreme state of fight or flight at that very instant.

That was then, and this is now. So what happens to you each and every time you relive, remember, re-enact scenarios or conversations, bump up against the hardest memories or guilt traps? What is your body doing now when you are confronted by the everyday issues surrounding this suicide and the life that existed with your loved one? Without utilizing guidance or intervening consciously, your breathing and heart rate systems are functioning and reacting under duress just like before, but to a different degree. It's no longer fight or flight; *it's a long-term storm watch.* If you are not interceding and adjusting for your body's health, you are simply coping; and you cannot imagine how much the human body can "cope," how high you can raise the bar over and over again until it reaches a limit or a wall. That limit or wall can be a dangerous obstacle to your wellbeing over the long haul. Perhaps you will recall the father I discussed in the previous chapter on Intention. I can only medically speculate what was happening to his body over the fourteen years of physically coping following his son Joel's suicide.

Let's discuss what constitutes deep breathing. (In various places in the book I will abbreviate it to DB.)

Some of you may know the answer to this, but many of you will not, since more than 90 percent of us breathe shallow and from the chest only, all day long. That's 20,000 or more shallow breaths every day. If we are not involving our abdomen, then we are sincerely cheating ourselves of diaphragmatic air and ultimately better health. By now you are saying to yourself—and believe me when I tell you that as I am writing this line, I can hear you! "This book is about surviving suicide loss— why do I care about my own breath? My dear loved one doesn't have their breath anymore, so why are we talking about this trivial topic?"

The answer is simple. If you have fears associated with suicide or otherwise, if you are angry about anything to do with your loved one and this situation, if you are terribly sad every single day and that sadness makes you come up short when you least expect it, you will improve your ability to overcome the barriers and challenges to healing your heart by drawing healing deep breath into your body at the moment you really need it.

By breathing deeply, you allow your body to engage the stressor coming to, or at, you, decrease your physical reaction to it, and therefore allow the brain tissues to get the oxygen and nutrition to help you get through to the other side of it.

We can either feed the very things we want the least (fear, anger, sadness, guilt) or we can sidestep and rise above it through effective deep breathing.

"Feelings come and go like clouds in a windy
sky. Conscious breathing is my anchor."

—Thich Nhat Hanh

First we should know and understand what constitutes
deep breathing, and then become familiar with the simple steps of the activity. Perhaps many of you have experience with what incorporates a deep breath because you
meditate, use a physical trainer, practice yoga, or possess
a medical background. Having the knowledge is wonderful, but knowing and practicing deep breathing repeatedly and consciously are often polar opposites in the course
of the day. So even if you know what you are doing here,
indulge me and read what it means to take a deep breath.
It helps to know that DB is considered by most health and
medical organizations as a true relaxation technique.

*"Diaphragmatic breathing, (also known as, abdominal
breathing, belly breathing or deep breathing) is breathing that
is done by contracting the diaphragm, the strong muscle located horizontally between the chest cavity and stomach cavity.
Air enters the lungs and the belly expands during this type of
breathing."* [1]

Lung expansion that is lower—deep within the abdominal cavity—is referred to as deep breathing. The
higher lung expansion of rib cage breathing is referred
to as shallow breathing.

The National Institutes of Health (NIH) resides within the U.S. Dept. of Health and Human Services, and is a wealth of current and extremely relevant information for us. A subgroup of NIH is the National Center for Complementary and Alternative Medicine (NCCAM). I found a wonderful article specifically about breathing and the serious connections that are now known to exist between stress and physical illness, and how the practice of various relaxation techniques may work to bring about better health.

"To understand how consciously producing the relaxation response may affect your health, it is helpful to understand how your body responds to the opposite of relaxation—stress. Under stress, your body releases hormones that produce the "fight-or-flight" response. Heart rate and breathing rate increase and blood vessels narrow (restricting the flow of blood). This response allows energy to flow to parts of your body that need to take action, for example the muscles and the heart. However useful this response may be in the short term, there is evidence that when your body remains in a stress state for a long time, emotional or physical damage can occur. Long-term or chronic stress (lasting months or years) may reduce your body's ability to fight off illness and lead to or worsen certain health conditions. In contrast to the stress response, the relaxation response (or in this discussion, deep breathing technique), slows the heart rate, lowers blood pressure, and decreases oxygen consumption and levels of stress hormones, thus counteracting the negative effects

of stress. This deep breathing is marked by expansion of the <u>abdomen</u> *rather than the* <u>chest</u> *when breathing."*

(National Center for Complementary and Alternative Medicine - NCCAM) [2]

So now that we understand what DB is and why it is important enough for me to make it one of the seven steps that formulate this book, let's learn a good and proper technique for practicing deep breathing.

DEEP BREATHING TECHNIQUE
An easy A-B-C-D method to deep breathe:

A. Find a comfortable position for yourself. You may sit in a chair, stand or be sitting on the floor. Place one hand on your upper chest, over your heart area, and the other hand resting on your stomach barely above the navel.

B. Begin taking a breath that comes from the belly area and feel the hand on your abdomen rise and fall. If the hand that is on your chest is having all the action when you inhale and exhale, then you are not yet using your abdomen primarily. Focus on the diaphragm doing the work, expanding outward.

C. Always breathe in through your nose. Keep your lips closed and take your time. A good count on inhalation is about 4 or 5. Breathe out through your lips slightly pursed, and do this to the count of 6 to 8.

D. Keep your mind as clear as possible of other thoughts. If you are paying attention to the breathing steps, it will remarkably keep you focused on the breathing procedure as opposed to extraneous interludes.

Learning the technique and practicing deep breathing is the start. If these steps are familiar, you are on your way to healthy living in stressful times. If you know the principles of DB but don't practice it, you are not alone, it happens to all of us. It simply means you won't be receiving its benefit until you do establish a practice. Why not get started by forming an Intention that will help you change your behavior, beginning today? (This is your first example of how the seven steps of healing will work together. Intention works with Breathing by helping you set a small desire for change and putting it into action. Deep breathing makes space for clarity and thus a meaningful intention. Sample intentions associated with breathing will be given as suggestions later in this section.

Below, are some guidelines for using deep breathing when you might need it the most – and it is often when you least expect it. I found that most of my stressful situations arose from my own mental state at the moment—perhaps I was having a particularly difficult day or encounter—when I felt fear, intense sadness or anger that surfaced outrageously fast and backed me into an emotional corner. I usually never saw these scenarios coming, but deep breathing gave me the edge I required to move through them in two important ways. First, my body received directly the perfect fuel (O2) for working properly, and secondly DB allowed for my emotions to shift in a way that brought understanding on how to handle a situation without overwhelming myself with an unwanted response.

THE PROCESS FOR DEEP BREATHING IN A CRUCIAL MOMENT

1. Stop what you are doing if at all possible. *If you are driving and you can pull over, do so. You really cannot do this safely if you are operating any vehicle or machinery.* I know this sounds almost silly, almost like a drug warning, but it's true. Your mind must focus on your breath, not what is going on around you.

2. If you are speaking with someone, pause, hold your conversation. They can wait. The entire world can wait while you take care of yourself.

3. Close your eyes if this helps you. Eventually, you will be able to DB anywhere at any time and your intended positive response will be the outcome. If you can close your eyes you are eliminating the movement and activity that enters your vision and periphery.

4. Arrest your thoughts and think only of the air moving through your body. If the fear, anger or pain seeps back in, gently put it aside for now and only "see" the air.

5. To assist in concentration of breath, it may help to give the air a color. You could visualize the intake air as being golden (or any color of your choice). Release white air (or any color of your choice). It reminds you that you are eliminating stress and negativity and sending it away from your body. In your mind, see it go skyward taking the fear/anger/sadness particles with it.

6. Breathe deeply using the A-B-C-D method. Do it again. Repeat as many times as you think you need to until you feel the positive effect.

7. Open your eyes and feel the calm return to your body/mind and spirit. Resume your conversation or activity, knowing full well you are mentally more present, and your brain and organs are getting the fuel they need to work properly, helping

to reduce your stress levels. You are now in a better place for whatever comes next.

Perhaps you are already experiencing physical symptoms that could be attributed to stress—acute, chronic or even long-term. Be alert to what you feel like physically each day. Is it possible that your body's response to stress has accelerated or increased with time since suicide loss became part of your life? Do you suspect your physical body responds negatively to specific activities, thoughts or people? Are you happy with how your physical body greets the day or retires at day's end? Are you willing to accept that doing a deep breathing exercise would help you be a less-stressed and a healthier individual without giving up huge amounts of time? Sincerely, what do you have to lose by accepting an opportunity to manage unwanted fear, anger and physical discomfort using a simple but effective approach?

It is a very tough pattern to break free of emotionally charged reactions to specific conditions or situations. Using deep breathing as a method to counter intense emotional response creates the way to decelerate and shift your coping to safe and manageable levels. Below are several situations survivors often encounter that revolve around fear and other stressors associated with our unique recovery. There are certainly many more that will be unique to you, but anything that concerns how we face fearful decisions, unexplained anger, panic, intense sadness, and feelings of guilt and isolation, are encounters you can recognize and treat with deep breathing—before, during and after the emotional upheaval.

REOCCURRING FEAR

Consider what it is like when you are confronted with some fear – an unexpected noise in the middle of the night, someone touching you on the shoulder when you didn't even know they were behind you, or the intense flood of feelings and emotions while watching a frightening movie. Temporary situations such as these are typical of the fight or flight syndrome, in which the body consistently responds appropriately and then adjusts to normal. *Long term fears that remain unresolved often return to affect the mind/body/spirit over and over again, and may contribute to unhealthy and potentially harmful physical conditions.* Deep breathing will always be available for you to combat the fears that threaten to derail your healing process.

Example situation 1

"Whenever I meet up with certain people, I know they are judging me and my deceased loved one as being inadequate, impaired, uncaring, selfish, wrong, even cowardly. I cannot go to that party or that holiday celebration because it will all rise up again and I can just hear them talking privately about my loved one and us. My heart rate goes straight through the roof, my belly and muscles are tense and actually become painful, and I have to interact with the very *people who make me feel so badly.* I need to avoid them at all costs."

Using deep breathing in this example:
You will be able to breathe through this fearful encounter and any anticipated encounters using the following methods. (Note: the steps actually involve another tool you have not yet encountered – Manifesting What You Think.)

* Whenever I think I am being "watched" because of my family's suicide history, I take several deep breaths, feel the fear response subside or lessen, then turn that thought into being gently "watched over."
* People may not know what to say, but I now choose to believe that they are sending their unspoken love and strength to my family and me, rather than disparaging our history.
* I will think: How wonderful that they care so much and want to help our journey by surrounding us with invisible arms. They are not blaming us; they are sending us silent blessings.

* If I am in fearful anticipation of a group meeting or get-together, I resolve to take quiet time prior to the event and deep breathe. I follow the guidelines for Intention-setting; I form an intention that states that fear and worry are not part of my thinking process about others who see me and speak with me. I make my intention a positive statement of what I desire.

* I see myself as being "watched over" by everyone I meet during this time. I enter the occasion with confidence. I am calm and prepared.

Example situation 2:

Another family member or friend, someone else within the inner Ring of Fire, shows what you consider signs of unabated sadness or possibly depression. You are aware that statistics have shown that the rate of suicide can be twice as high in families of suicide victims as in other families. You are already dealing with your own fragile state of mind, but now find yourself intensely worried about them. In the case of Drew, I do still agonize at times over what familial or community distress his children may experience as they grow up. What should we be watching for as they move from preschool to adolescent to teen? Is this a "disease" that can be inherited? How do I/we manage this fear when it looms so clearly in our mind?

Using deep breathing in this example:

Watching for signs of depression that may or may not come is like waiting for water to boil using a light bulb. It can feel like endless observation clouded by anxiety and anticipation of worse case scenarios. Sometimes it is simply because you are so intimately connected to suicidal loss yourself. Without getting a reasonable handle on your own fear, everything your family member does, says, or asks is suspect. Try the following:

* If a young child or someone else poses a question about suicide, this is the time to pause and take a DB before answering. Perhaps they just need to vent or wish to understand something that is difficult for them to grasp.

* Taking a DB will help to calm and clear your mind before you give your response, and can prevent you from entering panic mode when you really need to be in watchful mode.

* If you are worried about another survivor's condition, take a cleansing breath, and be a good and honest listener. If you see something that clearly disturbs you, say what you see, and ask if they need to seek some professional support.

* Sadness and depression may mimic each other. If you are not a licensed counselor, and most of us

are not, then suggesting they get medical advice makes perfect sense.

* Give people close to you a chance to help themselves. Use DB techniques and be present, not fragmented. Be the support, not the fear-filled fixer.

Example situation 3:

This is one of my personal stories. Every time I passed "the location" or even the geographical area where my son died, I was afraid and couldn't go near it. I was completely paralyzed to drive down that road or past that building. My fear actually extended to any place or spot that even reminded me of it. I was completely unable to look at the name of the town on the highway exit sign without becoming physically ill with fear. My mouth would dry up and nausea rose in my throat. *My heart rate accelerated so badly I was convinced I was having a heart attack.* I saw only painful memories there, not routine real estate! Has this happened to you as it did me? Short of moving out of town, selling my property, or changing jobs, I needed to create a way to manage my pain and anxiety surrounding it.

Using deep breathing in this example:

You are facing a difficult situation that surrounds a physical location. You can use your quiet time and DB to get you past the memories that accompany what you see in your mind. Use the clarity that comes with increased calm and brain function to formulate your action or in-action. Fear is being driven out with every exhalation you make.

* This is only a place, a physical location. No-one is telling you that you have to spend time there. If it is on your way to work and you must pass it frequently, see it on a daily basis or actually be within its confines, you will help yourself by deep breathing before you encounter it yet again.

* The golden light comes into you as you inhale, and the white light carrying the fear out of you as you exhale. DB will help you realize this space cannot hurt you.

* Set an intention that meets the needs of how you want to deal with the emotional and often physical responses that arise when you are near this location. Do this ahead of time—prepare. See your intention working in your body and see yourself being successful. Make your decisions involving spatial stressors by using DB and specific intention.

(For the full story of how I met my own challenge with this situation, I refer you to the step on Meditation/

Silence/Release and what I did to end my fear about the location.)

Example situation 4:
"Please don't make me go to that movie, that park, that vacation spot, that restaurant. That was my loved one's favorite and it *will make me feel sick at heart.* I know I will cry all the way through it. I will have a panic attack. I feel like I can't breathe."

Using deep breathing in this example:

This is another, even more common real estate issue, like the scenario above. The first two paragraphs are exactly the same technique.

* This is only a place, a physical location. No one is telling you that you have to spend time there. If it is on your way to work and you must pass it frequently, see it on a daily basis or actually be within its confines, you will help yourself by deep breathing before you encounter it yet again.
* Set an intention that meets the needs of how you want to deal with the emotions and often physical responses that arise when you are near this location. Do this ahead of time—prepare. See your intention working in your body and see yourself

being successful. Make your decisions involving spatial stressors by using deep breathing and specific intention.

1. What was it about the movie that they loved so much or made them laugh so hard? I can laugh through it and love it too, can't I? Build this into your intention.
2. If I order the same menu choice in the restaurant that they did, I can appreciate what a fine palette they had and why they continued to come and enjoy the dishes served. Build this into your intention.
3. I can always choose a different vacation spot if I wish, but I will not allow a location to hold me hostage – it is just a place. It is not a cause. Build this into your intention.

Recognize your triggers and put them on the table to see the situations and populations that induce your fear. By doing so, you omit the burying of feelings best examined and dealt with. By dealing with the emotional environment that the triggers produce, we get out ahead of the physical insult and move into health and healing.

LONG-TERM ANGER AND NEGATIVITY

Anger following any death is a normal reaction. It is generally self-limiting and recognizable as an emotional response in adjusting to loss, especially suicide. Long-term anger is a whole different animal entirely. This type of anger is unproductive, has a negative response on the body and its daily functioning. It can contribute to heart disease, high blood pressure, stress and panic attacks. This slow burning condition eventually isolates us from healthy social situations as well. Occasionally you may hear, (in reference to the survivor), the comments of: "He's never been the same since losing his loved one. He is really negative about everything now. I find it very hard to have a conversation with her because she seems so angry all the time. I get really uncomfortable when I am around her – she radiates negativity."

What follows are some of the situations we can find ourselves working through concerning perpetual anger or negativity. These thoughts or beliefs can be coming from you the survivor, or from someone else towards you. They may be spot-on with what you have experienced or close to it.

Scenario:

* Whenever I, the survivor, see the victim's family I am reminded that they/we didn't do enough to avoid this outcome. *If they or I had only just...*we

wouldn't be grieving right now. We could have stopped it; we could have intervened, we could have done something.

* I don't like hearing about someone else's success and happy interactions with their loved ones. Perhaps they just had a fabulous vacation with their mother/father, took their daughter to college for their first semester, received flowers for their anniversary from their spouse or were a witness for their best friend's wedding. I should have that. I should be doing those things. I can't bear for them to be happy when I cannot be happy myself.

* Whenever I think of how my lost loved one just "exited" I get furious about how selfish they were. I am pissed off that they just up and left the building! They have left us here to raise their children alone and take care of everything by ourselves. They removed any chance to interact with them ever again, and decimated our secured happiness for a lifetime. My *anger returns over and over again.* They had no right to make a decision that affected everyone around them.

* The doctors/practitioners are at fault. They missed all the signs of pending doom. If they had given the correct medications, if they had put them in a protected environment or institution, if they had taken more responsibility or a

deeper interest, my loved one would have been more stable and would not have done this. It has to be resting in their hands. *I blame them. I blame God. I blame everyone.*

Using deep breathing in these examples:

* Deep breathe through your inaccurate and angry rationale. As a survivor, it feels better to be able to point that finger and make someone be at fault for the whole situation. Allow that this response is normal to experience, but dangerous to hold on to.
* Set an intention that is a positive reflection of where you want to be regarding blame. Formulate a statement that will either address what you need to do next, or what you need to release because it is no longer worthy.
* We are all responsible for ourselves and we can be responsible for doing our very best to raise our own children; however, we cannot be responsible for the actions and intentions of another person, no matter who they are and what their relationship is to us.
* Set an intention about accepting only the responsibility that belongs to you. When the emotion of blame or guilt arises, use intention and

> deep breathing together as the calming action to anger.

* We would like to find the reasons why our loved one took their own life, but the fact remains that we probably will never know the "Why" of their actions. It is beyond our scope of human understanding. As hard as it is to say this; set the intention that states, *"I cannot fix someone else — I could not fix my loved one."*

* Deep breathe.

GUILT

Guilt, so similar in nature to long-term anger and negativity, is a silent but violent attack on our body/mind/spirit and, ultimately, our health. Guilt of any kind can be driven down deeply into recesses that we choose not to examine ever again, but rest assured, it continues to resurface over and over without resolution. Our heart cannot heal when it carries around the thought that the suicide of our loved one rests solely on our shoulders and we did nothing to stop it. This hindsight is awful to contemplate because we see ourselves as co-conspirators in their death, when actually it couldn't be further from the truth. As Drew's mother I have had to embrace the fact that there was only one person that was responsible for Drew's suicide and that was Drew.

The toughest job we have as a survivor is realizing when we misplace any blame for the outcome onto ourselves. By doing this, we are living an untruth. No one is to blame, and only one person is responsible. If you have regrets of any kind, you are automatically aligning yourself with guilt. After Drew's death, I circled around many of these regrets, irrationally speculating on what might have happened if I had only:

- Returned his phone call sooner
- Driven by his house
- Given him my full attention the week before
- Not gone on vacation
- Looked in the medicine cabinet and counted his pills to see if he was taking them
- Helped him find a better job
- Seen the sadness in his eyes
- Loaned him the money
- Let him come and live with us
- Not had that argument last month
- Driven him to the doctors myself
- Found the hidden meaning in his last phone text
- Asked him the questions... Are you depressed? Do you need to see someone professionally? Are you contemplating hurting yourself?

Using your deep breathing in answer to your mind's interrogation:

* If you have regrets you are aligned with guilt. Take your deep breathing and settle into a relaxed mental and physical posture. State the intention, "I Am Guilt-Free." Say it for the moment, say it for the day, say it to yourself or to anyone else who indicates otherwise. Live this intention as deeply as you can, because it is the hardest one to believe in for any survivor of suicide loss.

* Self-imposed guilt is the number one lingering tragedy for the survivor. As you deep breathe, declare "I Am Guilt-Free." This allows you to grieve without investing in the outcome. If your mind begins to waver in the face of guilty thoughts, believe in your practice.

* You can miss your loved one and be sad, but it will be temporary. If you don't develop the strategy for it now it will be with you for a lifetime. Get the breath in you and release the guilt with the air of (white) exhalation. It doesn't belong to you, so you need to make it gone.

SADNESS AND DEPRESSION

We all know what sadness is firsthand. The loss of a loved one by any means, suicide or otherwise, produces mental anguish and sadness at what we no longer have. Now let me clarify that sadness beyond what you might term "understandable under the circumstances," sadness that continues to be present for months without relief, clinical depression, the inability to get up out of bed after a full night's rest and similar descriptions, should always be discussed with your physician. If it doesn't feel right, even to you, then it probably isn't and medical care should be sought. Overwhelming sadness incapacitates an individual, and true depression needs to be evaluated and treated. This book was not written to diagnose, and I am not a mental health practitioner.

That being said, I will declare that there are moments that I feel true sadness at my loss, and I probably always will. I am a human and humans experience sadness; that is how we are designed. I let it come and wash over me and it makes me realize that with this emotion I am alive! I don't need to apologize to anyone for it. So, I will weep at a song that brings me sweet memories of Drew, and I will shed tears when I see a pair of hands that look just like his; beautiful, strong and lean, like those of a pianist. The difference for me is that my tears will inevitably bring the corners of my mouth up in a smile. Before I let the feeling overwhelm me, I take a deep breath and then I smile. That breath will turn me around, nearly every time.

Using your deep breathing to manage sadness:

* This is your chance to recognize, honor and stabilize your sadness due to loss. Welcome the emotion; give it the encounter and time it needs, but breathe through it. The gold air in and the white air out are creating the healing environment for your next thought and your next step. It will never ever make it worse; it can only make it better and give you strength to move along in your healing journey.

* If you find that an unexpected sadness strikes you at a moment when you are not alone or in a private space, you can choose not to expose your emotional state publicly. Stop what you are doing, pause your conversation and deep breathe. Whatever is going on can wait while you take care of yourself. If you are comfortable expressing your sadness where you are, then do so. Soon enough you will be ready to deep breathe and feel the relaxation soothe your physical and mental self.

* When sadness arises, and your deep breathing successfully stabilizes you, take the time at some

point to examine where the sadness came from and what made it manifest. Here is how you recognize some of the triggers that set your emotions in motion. This is not a bad thing you need to address or fix; it just helps you learn something about yourself and your relationship to the healing process. Use it to your advantage.

Allow me to offer a personal example of how to do this. On several occasions I have mentioned my son Drew's beautiful hands. About one year after Drew died, my dear friend and I were taking a day trip and we visited a lovely chapel across the state. Unexpectedly, a young priest walked from the back of the chapel up the aisle with his hands extended outward in a welcoming gesture. I practically stopped breathing—the hands I was looking at belonging to the priest, were Drew's! Everything about them was familiar. My sadness was overwhelming and devastating. I wept uncontrollably, bowing my head; I was totally losing touch with the moment. Then I took many deep and wonderfully cleansing breaths. The next thing I realized was that I was still staring at the priests hands, so in motion now, and was truly fascinated! How beautiful it all was. It was as if Drew sent this man into my life for a few minutes to remind me about the magnificence of the human body, and sweet reminders of those we loved the most. Setting my intention was easy—I will always be watching gratefully for Drew's hands to suddenly appear when I least expect it.

THE PRACTICE

* Teach yourself ways to recognize your deep breathing moments. Are you aware of your triggers? Try listing them out ahead of time: music, photographs, certain conversations, certain people, their birthday/anniversary/wedding day and holidays.

* Keep a pulse (pardon the pun here) on your body systems. Do you know when your blood pressure is going up by the way you feel during an encounter? Put some thoughts into how your pulse and heart beat are changing if you are nervous, angry, feeling sad or guilty. DB is the perfect antidote to unhealthy symptoms you recognize.

* Set an Intention for using deep breathing. Example: I make time each day upon arising to do deep breathing just for myself.

* Practice DB as many times during the day as you want or can, either with a specific incident or simply as practice for your improved health. When you need to rely on DB for something

unexpected, it will be as familiar to you as possible.

* Always check to see that you are following the proper steps to DB. When you re-read and practice, you are cementing your understanding of how air moves through your body effectively.

* Set a training reminder. Make it fun; be creative about how you remind yourself. For instance, DB whenever you:

> * See something green
> * Enter a building
> * Get into your car
> * Finish brushing your teeth
> * Complete a phone call

* Compliment yourself for deep breathing during the day or at any time. Smile after you practice and remember that this doesn't require going to the gym and getting on the treadmill. Congratulate yourself for improving your health and releasing your stress!

CHAPTER 4

Gratitude and Appreciation

(It's All Abundance)

*"Gratitude can turn a negative into a positive.
Find a way to be thankful for your troubles
and they can become your blessings."*

— AUTHOR UNKNOWN

I SUSPECT THAT FEELING GRATITUDE and appreciation for many things has sort of left the building for you. Perhaps you are not expecting to really appreciate much of anything now and for some time to come. After all, the impact of such tragedy has a tendency to remove the ability to recognize gratitude very well. There is no blame here for this cognitive loss, it just happens that way. Coping in any form is difficult. The question is, does it need to stay that way or can it be changed by gaining a different perspective? Within a split second it seems any situation in which we find ourselves can bring to mind our loss, and instantly become painful and unbearable to think about. It can often be the simplest encounter or environmental influence. How can we possibly change our perspective when the conditions of our thoughts are repeatedly inviting anger, guilt and fear?

On the other hand, a change in perspective may give you some unexpected relief. Defining gratitude is probably different for everyone. What really constitutes being grateful and to what degree? In my book, grateful is 180 degrees away from angry or negative. It doesn't seem to me that we can be grateful for something and be pissed off at the same time. You might try to make a case here to the contrary, but I don't see it as working. You *can* however be grateful for your anger; perhaps it is telling you or teaching you something you have heretofore missed. Maybe you are not quite seeing that yet, but your anger can spark change for which you are grateful. Get it? You simply step back and look at your emotional responses and find opportunities for change that you appreciate and are willing to try.

Recently I had the chance to return to my old neighborhood where I grew up, in a state quite far from where I live now. Fifty years had transpired since I had seen it last. Talk about change! And the crazy thing is the streets were still there, with the same names, but many of the residences had altered. I tried to feel my childhood embrace me again, but the newness interfered – the grade school I walked to every day was gone, my old homestead was tiny, the gang of friends was long departed and unable to welcome me back in. A large part of me was sad and actually angry by the changes that had taken place. Nothing I saw would ever be the same again; it was lost to me and I could never go back. I will never have that world exist again for me ever. I looked around me and said, "Hey, what the hell happened to those days and places I loved so much?"

Is this starting to sound familiar? Because of suicide and loss, we have moved away from a life we knew and were perhaps naively safe in, and are now unwillingly facing a change that we never wanted to make or see. We cannot go back there and find it just the way it was. That life is totally gone from us. Often we feel devastatingly remorseful and thoroughly, permanently pissed off. We have lost a lot.

Back in my neighborhood, I also saw something else. In the middle of the old stuff was some interesting and wonderful new stuff. The school had made way for a beautiful and green walking park and playground; the dumpy building where I bought my first illegal cigarette as a teen — don't fret, I stopped trying smokes shortly after getting that first one — was now a sweet Mom and Pop market with fresh fruit and household needs. My original church was in the same location, had expanded its buildings and parking areas to accommodate a larger parish, but still kept the old ambiance of the original style.

Buried within the tragedy of our loss there are some elements of understanding and knowledge that we can recognize and perhaps cling to; something to appreciate and be grateful for. If we are angry and guilt-ridden we will not find them. In any given moment identifying them becomes our challenge. Are you ready to do that?

CHANGING OUR PERSPECTIVE

Let's try looking at something very common that we all know just for an illustration. Do you remember the first time you rode a merry-go-round or a carousel? If you never have ridden one, just go along with the image here, since you know what it does. Let's say you were small enough to enjoy the ride and old enough to ride alone. Some adult or parent or guardian stood on the ground off the platform as a pillar or placement by which you could always get your bearings as you went around and around. They were the "anchoring" you could identify with. After you passed by them, you entered the outer regions of the ride, better known as the "other side." What was there for you to see as you moved by places that didn't contain your anchors? Perhaps it was unfamiliar anchors that belonged to other riders or tents and vendors you had not ever visited before, maybe even a parking area that was big and wide and a little scary. Not to worry, in a short few seconds you were passing your folks, and all was familiar again.

You can make that merry-go-round circle as big or small as you want, but the fact remains that directly opposite your known anchor exists a robust thought, idea and perspective not yet observed nor considered. If your anchors are resentment, negativity, guilt, blame and fear, just stay on your horse and you will simply end up right back where you started. Is that what you want? Is that healing you?

Why not test this discussion with a real issue in your healing journey? You have just run across a photo of a group of friends, with you and your loved one right in the center of the picture. Everyone is smiling and laughing, it was a picture perfect day. As you gaze at this picture, you can't believe how fast the sadness and anger swells up in you – the joy you are observing in the photo will never happen again in your lifetime. You ask yourself, why in the world did I find this photo? I cannot bear to see their face staring back at me because they took it all away in a moment—this hurts so terribly.

In theory, let's ride to the opposite regions of the carousel, directly across from the familiar anchors of anger and painful sadness. This view holds a fully new perspective. What an incredible day that was in the picture. You all were having the most glorious experience of love and friendship, fun and bonding. Your loved one's beaming face is reflecting pure joy and you want to hold that to your heart as a wonderful memory. You were a better person because of that day and so were they. Your emotional reaction at the other side of the merry-go-round concerning this photo is completely different from what you started with; it reflects a mirror image to your sadness and anger and becomes the joy and appreciation of a day wonderfully spent together. This is gratitude. It is healthy and it is healing.

Perhaps your grateful thoughts can't go quite that distance, so why not think of something that demonstrates you are moving in the right direction? Maybe the location in the photo, the place you all enjoyed so much is worth another visit. You can go there with a friend and mentally revisit the laughter and the event more peacefully and in your own pace. Another solution might be to take the photo, put it in a lovely frame, and set it on your writing desk where you can see it every day and give a smile every time you pass by it.

Let's try another example that involves gratitude. You are thinking about your loss and how your ability to be a part of a full life has been taken from you. Suicide removed all chances of that in a moment's decision. The unfairness is consuming you.

In this instance, ride away from the familiar anchors of loss and try to embrace the new perspectives. You had this extremely important person in your life for all that time before they died. If this was your child, you carried them in your womb or your arms, enduring colic and sleepless baby nights. If this was your best friend, you shared countless experiences together that bonded you. If this person was a parent or sibling, they gave you love and guidance and helped make you the person you are today. In my case I had Drew for forty-one incredible and gifted years. To me that is a better thought than suffering with regret at what I no longer have. If these declarations seem too far to reach right now, then try to say, "I am sending my loved one an enormous hug right now and they are hugging me right back." Experience it. Feel it if you can. If this is still too deep a stretch, place a smile on your face and picture a smile on theirs – share that smile right over eternity's airwaves. Tomorrow it will be easier to ride a little further.

ABUNDANCE

Recognizing abundance in all of its forms tales effort as a survivor. It requires looking beyond the material and the face value and finding the lesson and the great gift of understanding. If it truly helps us in the long run, whether we see it or not at the time of receiving, then it is abundance in its purest form.

Most often the form of abundance does not represent money, acquisitions or power. More likely abundance comes in the form of a gift or action that may not always feel comfortable when it first arrives. My daughter Emma was recently laid off from her position within a large organization, along with many others in her department. As you can imagine, Emma's self-confidence was sincerely shaken and the confidence she had built up over the last several years sort of imploded. A month or so before the news was delivered to departmental staff, a young man from the Eastern part of the globe came to work as a contractor with my daughter's department. While his English was somewhat labored, he was extremely articulate, and he readily shared his country's customs and mores. He was full of good humor and intelligence, and always appreciative of the mentoring and assistance he received at the hands of the staff, especially Emma. As my daughter's time drew near to leave the department for the last day, this young man took the opportunity to tell her how much he treasured her guidance and training, telling her that her knowledge freely given meant the world to him. What a gift. Emma's self- assurance and confidence were boosted beyond measure by that conversation and acknowledgment, directly in the face of a lay-off. *That* is abundance.

A PERSONAL STORY OF GRATITUDE

There is a local haunt that my son Drew and his friends would frequent, often featuring a band and guitarist — part of their high school crowd — that they grew up with and loved. Many nights were spent in laughter and storytelling, dancing and karaoke. Drew was always smack in the middle of it all, singing with his buddies on stage. Three months after his passing, these loving friends had a fantastic fundraiser for the family, and the pounding drumbeat and noise could be heard blocks away. I believed it would be far too painful to go and I came within moments of cancelling out my appearance. What right did anyone have to make any kind of merriment when my suffering was so profound that it was interfering with my entire life?

In the end, I went anyway. I will always remember the joyful abundance that day brought to all of our lives. I couldn't believe how grateful I felt at such giving and love and appreciation for my son's existence. The pounding music literally broke the sound barrier up and down the street. What I thought would appall me, crush me, bring me to my knees, brought me such happiness instead. There were young people dancing on the bar, clapping hands, making generous donations to benefit his children, and sharing stories about Drew. I learned so much about my son and his friendships that day and I had a great deal to be grateful for in just a few hours! How unexpected! How healing!

Almost three years to the day later, I ran across the wife of one of the band members in a restaurant and she invited us to attend another gig at the same bar and grill that evening. Many of Drew's friends were there again and by the end of the night I was full of the energy and love that only this kind of remembrance and joy can produce. What a gift—who would have ever thought? If you are open to recognize gratitude and abundance of any sort especially when it surrounds your loved one, it will open your heart to healing, every time.

Community support groups and organizations, as well as the medical community, can be just several of many avenues of abundance. If you are drawn to share your journey with others who are going through the same experience of loss, then a short research into your local listings may be the very thing to give you strength in numbers. These groups are not necessarily right for everyone, but try them once or twice and make your own decisions about continuing. We belong to a unique club that no one asked to be in, but taking advantage of the experiences of others leaves a great deal to be grateful for and aids in our own healing process. One of the amazing benefits to sharing with others in our situation is to find that they can provide an answer to some of our most delicate questions. Additionally, you might just give relief and support through something you say and know to another hurting and sad individual.

(Note: To find local support groups within your area, I refer you to the Resource and Reference section for website connections on Suicide Prevention and Survivor Support Groups.)

LEGAL ISSUES

Nothing can be more horrifying than losing someone to suicide and then finding out that you have no financial benefits that will be granted to you. Perhaps you must battle with the insurance company legally to get monies to meet your additional expenses and it is bumping right up against the reduced income you are now facing. If the legal impact of life insurance coverage is overwhelming or causing you mental stress, know that some life insurance clauses exist to protect you and your family more than they did a few years ago. Don't assume that no one is in your corner for legal help surrounding suicide. Guidelines for coverage regarding suicide loss within a family have changed in the last few years and influenced the written policies of insurance companies across America. Once written, insurance corporations are obligated to honor their policies. Also be aware that many organizations will expand their policies out of generosity to assist you when you need it the most. This new dimension becomes an opportunity for abundance we didn't know we had available to us. Any abundance received is abundance to be grateful for and appreciative of. Make a strong connection with someone in your insurance company – keep their number close at hand if you require frequent advice. Show them you are working gratefully with them and appreciate any and all help they can give you. People want to help, sometimes they just don't know how to until you tell them. Involve close friends, family lawyers and other professionals to be your advocates. Don't ever assume you need to do this alone. Appreciate the fact you have a lot of people in your corner, and while they have difficulty talking about or empathizing with your unique grief, they may want to help in a myriad of other ways for which they are capable. Use these associates as well and experience the appreciation in your heart. It is healing in and of itself.

Finding Abundance, Gratefulness and Appreciation on a daily basis

Celebrating your loved one on special occasions

Did you ever watch the movie with John Travolta called *Phenomenon?* At the end of the film, everyone got together for his birthday exactly one year after his death. It was such a joyous appreciation of his life and recognized the impact that he had made on the individual lives of his friends. What abundance. What a sense of gratefulness for having known him.

Why should we allow our loss to shed all value of a life lived when it involves future celebrations with our family, our friends or the community? The people in *Phenomenon* would have rather had a different outcome if that were possible and so would we, but no one of us could have anticipated this outcome. So why not turn our challenges around to embrace abundance and gratitude?

After our loss of Drew, we celebrated his birthday when it came around the first time. We made three different birthday cakes, decorated them with jimmies, sprinkles, hearts, way too much frosting and nearly eighty candles all lit at once. It took us three tries to keep the flames going at the same time and nearly set off the fire alarms. Next we put on his favorite music and songs and danced in the kitchen. The tears ran freely on all of our faces, but we did it with joy knowing Drew would have done the same thing given the chance. We probably won't continue that indefinitely, and I don't see that as abandonment, it is simply moving forward. In our family, we are choosing to find opportunities to participate in fund-raising events that are close to his death date. This is an effort to "Pay-it-Forward" for someone in need and we do it in Drew's memory. Is that not just one more way of generating appreciation, gratitude and abundance in the face of loss?

MEMORIES, PHOTOS, ARTIFACTS

What sort of talents and abilities did your loved one have? How did you appreciate their gifts when they were living that you can now appreciate still? Did they fund-raise by biking? Did they coach little league? Were they active in AA or other self-help groups? Can you share your abundance with others through donations, attendance, cheerleading, walking, riding and knowing that their legacy is continuing? While it feels difficult the first few times around, it just gets easier as time goes on because of all the people who benefit. Remember earlier I mentioned how the hole in our heart could be softened around the edges? It can also be slowly and surely filled with wonderful thoughts and ideas as well as memories of marvelous moments from the past and abundance for the future. How better to heal and fill that empty space with gratitude, rather than anger and bitterness?

Drew's paintings and drawings will forever reflect his incredibly creative soul, so we have them hanging wherever we can and show them to others for their appreciation and understanding of his massive talent. My daughter resurrected old photos that displayed the incredible affection and connection she had with her brother right from the start of her life. Looking at the photos and pointing out the funny, loving, memories of the then-moments truly shows the appreciation we share for our lives together. She constructed the arrangement of the pictures in such a way that they can be used as screen-savers on our computers. When I boot up, Drew and Emma show up. His beautiful face is forever shining back at me and reminding me that he had a loving relationship with us all right from beginning.

PENNY FOR MY THOUGHTS

Only two days after Drew passed, I was walking through his bathroom and there, sitting on the counter around his personal sink, was a penny. I could see him placing it there, out of his pocket at the end of his day, meaning to pick it up later. I took it in my hand and felt his energy. At that moment I felt so grateful that I was able to identify *that* penny as *his* penny, without any doubt in my mind. I have a small Indian medicine pouch that I wear from time to time around my neck and so that is where it resides. Whenever I seem to need Drew's counsel or creative input, I simply slip it over my head and his very presence seeps through to me. I often wore it as I was writing this book; it seemed to allow me to accurately express and scribe my — and his —knowledge, and therefore gain a foothold on our approach to life after suicide. I felt that it helped me to be a better author and composer.

THE TWO COBBLESTONES
Drew was forever puttering in his backyard with stone and patterned layouts for a patio. His OCD obviously made placement of certain cobblestones never "quite right" and they were moved over and over again with the intention of finding the perfect location. Looking over these placed, misplaced and replaced cobbles, I chose two of them I was certain that Drew had handled more times than anyone could ever count. I took them home, and being the gardener that I am, decided to create a quiet meditation space in his memory. Eventually

I placed these two large cobbles heralding the entrance to a beautiful garden spot, so that every time I walk between them I enter a silent and peaceful world. The gratitude and appreciation I feel in this location is almost beyond words. I feel that whoever rests there in the garden is sharing the wealth of his creativity and life purpose. In other words, we are all rejoicing at Drew's contribution to our lives – his brilliant analytical mind, his artistry and charismatic personality. What a grateful expression of love. It's not a shrine; it is a peaceful memory that goes on to benefit others.

PRESERVING THE MEMORIES WITHOUT TAGGING ON
DISASTROUS HINDSIGHT

On that first day of college so far from home, as I stood on the balcony of my hotel, I watched Drew drive out of the parking lot ten floors below me. Registration and orientation were over at this point and it was time for me to fly back home and let him move on with his extended education and new environment. I had asked him to stick his hand out of the driver's side window and wave at me as he passed out of our family unit into a whole new world of academics. What I saw were four fingertips barely making it out of the edge of the glass and scarcely moving – forget waving! He was frightened, alone and on his own. It was one of those times when, as a mother, a parent, you make a tough decision about "letting them go and letting them grow." What the hell was I doing? Leaving him to his own devices 3000 miles away from everything he knew and everything that was safe. This kid had never even been to camp for a week in his life and I was deserting him to a huge party school where he didn't know one person and didn't have one friend on campus. I cried all the way home on the plane; so hard and so loud that people surreptitiously moved away from the row I was in. I didn't want to be around me, why would they?

Drew called almost every night, nearly in tears and told me he was eating alone, talking to no one and no one was talking to him. "Puleez!" he begged me, "let me come home!" I listened to his fears, I answered his concerns the best I could, I encouraged him to stretch his social skills...and still he called home. Finally, I decided to give him a goal to reach for, and if it was unattainable by December break, he could come home to stay. Together we would re-define his academics and desires if this could not work out. We made a deal and he accepted it thinking that all he had to do was wait it out until Christmas.

Somewhere in late fall he decided to pledge a fraternity. He started meeting young men and women that thought and felt as he did. He was busy with pledge activities, events, socials and homework. The calls to home got farther and farther apart, and then they stopped altogether. When he finally came home at Christmas, I didn't recognize the mature adult before me. He was confident, happy and loved his school. The friends that he made in the first three months of college were so deep and so solid that after they all graduated from college, they visited each other all over the country and in some cases, other parts of the world. These very same "brothers" and those friends that he grew up with from high school stood next to me as we all said goodbye to him for the last time. Did he have friends who loved him, looked up to him, saw him as a role model, a super achiever, handsome, successful, brilliant, even lucky? The answer is an overwhelming, yes. He was everything in their eyes and ours. And yet, he held that undetectable, hidden secret that we all seemed to miss, and we were unable to identify him as being a human being in serious trouble.

I can look back on his high school and college years as such a gift for both him and us as a family. His ability to grow and become the adult young man who made us so proud had its footing in learning to adjust to new and often stressful situations and then running with it. Somewhere along the line of his life, those growth adjustments turned into strife and loss of self-esteem. No one was at fault. No one walked behind Drew and told him that if he wasn't careful he could become a monumental failure. He wasn't a failure in anyone's eyes, least of all his family's or friends' or co-worker's. Only in his own mind.

How many of us are scouring our past and the earlier years of our loved ones and deciding it was *here* or *there* that things started falling apart? How many times are we attempting to identify the precipitating event or moment that switched their thinking from unlimited success to monumental failure? This is what I call "Disastrous Hindsight" and it is the greatest waste of time you can spend. As I look back at the story I just told you of Drew's magnificent turnaround at college, I see the endless push of the human spirit to better one's condition. We are hopeful, we are open to change and improvement and we see significant possibilities to altering our thinking for the better. This is what gratitude and appreciation is all about. We don't need to stay in the empty place we find ourselves, just as Drew found that his academic experience would expand to include new friends and phenomenal changes if he just didn't stay in his lonely place. He had a way out by December if he chose to take it, but he never used it because he moved away from loneliness and reached out to the unknown instead.

Every young man I hug today will be Drew

On some days I miss Drew's presence so much I know that if I don't do something to turn my sadness to the other side of the merry-go-round, it could very well swallow me up. When this happens I have tried to find appreciation for Drew in every aspect of my day – I make the effort in ways people might not ever think of. Whenever I get the chance to hug a young man for whatever reason—and I can make the reason if I want to—I am hugging Drew. When I hug the gentleman in question, I close my eyes and hug my son. Before you label this as just a bit over the top, I would like to mention the movie *Ghost* when Whoopi Goldberg's character offered to step into the place of family members who had passed on. For just a few minutes, the hopeful family could experience their loved ones physical presence. The ghost, although deceased, had the experience, as well. In my hug, I see Drew feeling his mom giving one of her famous hugs once again, and so do I. In my heart I am making a physical connection, using someone else to receive it in his heart, and then passing it along to Drew. I can do that all day long and no one knows the difference, but I am healed immensely during those times. It is also my feeling that the person I am really hugging also receives benefit from the hug connection. Who knows, perhaps that is exactly what they needed for some reason at that very moment. The love is strong enough to cross all the dimensional barriers for the three of us.

The Practice

What are you grateful for, right this minute? I know you want to heal your heart beginning today, so get a pad of paper and pen, or sit yourself down at your computer and initiate a list. Perhaps you can only create a list of incidences that occurred today, and that is a fine place to start. What happened today to make you grateful even if it only lasted for a few moments? The following examples do not necessarily reflect anything related to suicide survival, but what they do highlight is the fact that grateful thinking and action is a learned skill. When you need to apply it to our unique healing journey, gratefulness, abundance and appreciation will come easier to you, simply because you have been practicing.

* Did you get a parking space really close to your building? And was it raining really hard outside? It's not too soon to recognize the ability to combine more than one tool. When the parking space materializes, say "Thank you," out loud. Who are you saying it to? Anyone you want, but mean it. Set an intention: Each time I need a parking space, I will ask my loved one to give me a hand in finding it.
* Did you receive something you weren't expecting to get until next week? Picture in your mind what it must have taken to get this item into your hands. People working together as a team; individuals dedicated to the highest quality in performing their job. Appreciate their honest hard

work on your behalf. All thoughts of gratitude and appreciation are being recorded in your consciousness as positive impressions. This is very healing and moves you away from negativity.

* Did a friend or relative call you and you hadn't heard from them in a really long time? Did you have a great conversation that lasted an hour? This is a form of celebration of yourself and those that care about you in this life. By honoring relationships, you honor what is good and loving in every day we exist.

* Did you make that important bank deposit just in time before it closed? Realize that a positive thought produces a positive outcome. Each time you feel a time management pressure, see the outcome as you would like it to be. You appreciate that the bank has specific hours and you are grateful that you were given leeway in the tight time frame. When it happens, say thank you. All are gifts of abundance.

* Did dinner taste exceptionally delicious? Consider that your body is miraculous and can experience good food and its flavors. Find gratitude for this simple pleasure.

* Was there a small green leaf on that little plant that you were sure was not going to make it? Why not see all living plants and creatures as part of

our amazing world and working as a team within it. See positive possibilities in what appears to be hopeless. See only success even in the smallest of things.

* Did you appreciate something as simple as a refreshing glass of water when you were thirsty from working outside in the hot sun? Simply say thank you in gratitude for what you are privileged to have in this country. Appreciate what good and healthy water tastes like. Abundance is that you have clean water to drink anytime you turn on the tap!

* Did you hear your loved one's favorite song play on the radio? Oh-oh. Were you grateful for that, too...or not? I hope you were. You absolutely can be. Surprise reminders such as this are little messages and whisperings to us from those who have passed.

You can express your gratitude as far back into time and space as you wish. Whatever feels right for you is right for you; just remember, being grateful is a giant step towards healing that place in your heart that is so broken. In the minute you are grateful, you cannot be angry or fearful at the same time.

"Gratitude bestows reverence, allowing us
to encounter everyday epiphanies, those
transcendent moments of awe that change
forever how we experience life and the world."

—JOHN MILTON

CHAPTER 5

Silence and Meditation

(Part I)

"Divide the constant tide and random noisiness
of energetic flow, with conscious recurring
moments of empty mind, solitude, gratitude
and deep...slow...breathing. Of this, the
natural law of self-preservation demands."

—T. F. HODGE

"Silence is a true friend who never betrays."

—CONFUCIUS

DURING THE POST-SUICIDE GRIEVING PERIOD, our mind
often struggles with the non-stop bombardment of
Things and *Thoughts*. *Things* that we are doing, have

108

done, must do; an endless list perpetuated out of daily necessity. At times it involves *Things* that others are doing, which can be good and not so good. And then the *Thoughts* of how to accomplish it all take over. Just like beautifully thin tracing paper, we overlay this *Doingness* onto the ever-present emotional connection to loss. Some examples of "doing" can be: professional work, obligations, the running of a household, relationships, child care, elder care, economics, illness and more. Recovery and healing survivorship is often pushed down and buried under tons of things and thoughts because dammit, it's easier. *"I would rather not face grief, because when I least expect it, my memories or 'triggers' break through and throw me."* In my energy work, I can actually feel the chaotic chatter and complex movement beneath someone's forehead when I hover over their brow. This is nonstop brain craziness that they are completely unable to let go of or control. And that could be on their best day.

Silence and meditation are forever connected to me. There are hundreds of ways to meditate. Perhaps you already have your own way of meditating, and I'll wager that every time you quiet your mind, by whatever means you use, you are in healing mode. Many of us do not use meditation, silence or mindfulness anywhere in our daily routine. We will declare that we don't really know how to quiet our minds and environment, it's complicated, and frankly, we don't have the time. Dear Reader, we are not shooting for Nirvana here. What we really want to do is to provide our minds and bodies a chance to have a voice – from the inside out. Most of the voices we receive are bombarding us from the outside in. Let's change that and start listening to ourselves and our inner guidance instead of simply reacting to all the noise from everywhere else.

Can we consider interrupting the *Doing-ness* and embrace the *Being-ness* that comes with silence or mindfulness, instead? For those of you who work or live in stressful situations –ones that can be a trigger for your anxiety, PTSD, sadness or other symptoms – stop, shut your door, any door, and get silent. Everyone gets a break somewhere in their waking hours, and you can find a spot that allows you to exercise your right to be still. Lean back, close your eyes, deep breathe and welcome the stillness. If your negative or worrying thoughts intrude, gently put them aside for consultation later. Take a walk without any electronics of any kind, not even a music playlist. Give your brain twenty minutes off. Just choose silence as one of your treatments to health and you will always find the when and the where.

INTERRELATEDNESS OF SILENCE AND MINDFULNESS

Silence – "the absence of sound," is so much more than just the lack of vibration to the cochlea. Silence can bring a much desired stillness and calm to the mind. I know this doesn't sound very original, but I love to call it Still-Mind. It is accomplished through the elimination of noise and thought, while focusing on somewhat of a blank slate in your head. It is a more concentrated reduction of what we normally experience. This practice can influence the body, the environment around us and even the breath in the most positive way. It removes the ability to evaluate, as well as judge. It supports the inner voice, rather than the human voice. Achieving silence and mindfulness can look very much, from the outside observer, as nearly the same. The difference lies within the internal climate of the person as they do it.

Mindfulness is gained by focusing our awareness on only the present moment. During mindfulness we can quietly acknowledge that our body is functioning normally through touch, sight, smell and other sensations. Mindfulness acknowledges that thoughts continue to come and go, but does not involve problem-solving or anxiety. It is all part of the process of being totally present, being still and observing.

In giving an example of both silence and mindfulness meditation, I will say that an individual practicing silence may see a candle behind their closed eyes, watch the flickering light, deep breathe at intervals, and "see" only the soft charcoal gray space in their minds eye. They may receive quiet, non-intrusive, positive insights without calling to them. The mindfulness experience is purposeful. They might be sitting barefooted on a park bench, recognizing how cool and soft the grass is on the soles of their feet, notice how warm their cheeks are from the sun on their face, and listen to a chick-a-dee calling in the tree beside them. They smile at how good it all feels, breathing deeply of the air that moves around and through them. *Silence is checking out and mindfulness is checking in.*

There is only preference that separates the mindfulness meditation from the silence meditation. What works for you is what you can choose to try. Try both. Either one will give your entire body what it needs the most – release from stress and a dose of healthy living. How I wish I could have taught Drew to practice meditation of any kind before he left us. I can see now that suicide is the antithesis of mindfulness. Perhaps it would have made a difference for him and how he might have coped within his day.

Just recently I had a gentleman stop at my curbside and decide to pick up a lawn sweeper that I was setting out free to anyone who wanted it. Since I was standing in my driveway and observed him pulling up next to the item, I introduced myself. He said to me that he knew who I was from others who have seen the gardens on my property and since he took my street frequently, he had always wanted to see them himself. Being in the now moment, I offered to take him in the back to look around. He asked me what it meant to have peaceful gardens, and I told him that I designed spaces for people to meditate and quiet their minds. Now, I wish to say that this man, at first glance, did not appear to be a meditator straight off. To my surprise he said that in his line of work he often had to deal with individuals that could be very difficult to get along with. He went on to say, that to put his mind in a position of calm, he had established an empty room in his house that only had a chair in it. He would go and sit in that chair with the door closed and bring healthy, peaceful and positive thoughts to his mind for 15 to 20 minutes each day. Wow, who knew? Is that meditating? Absolutely!

For some, silence is more of a curse than a gift. Many of us have to have some form of stimulation, auditory or otherwise, bombarding us all of the time – we simply cannot exist in a silent world. We jog with earbuds, stroll with cell phones, communicate incessantly without taking a breath, and run the flat screens without interruption even on the treadmill. Where is the break? Where are the intercessions? I love the synonyms of silence: quietness, quiet, quietude, stillness, hush, tranquility, noiselessness, soundlessness, peace, peacefulness. Honestly, when and where do we use these anymore? What are we teaching ourselves, our children, when it comes to silence?

Each time I introduce a new tool, I suspect you ask yourself about its application to your recovery, and that is a fair question surrounding the tool of Silence, Meditation and Release. I didn't choose these steps lightly; they exist because they have helped to save my psyche and move my healing process forward, always and without exception. While meditation comes in many forms, the practice that has helped me the most is Still-Mind. I combine Intention, Breathing and Silence and find the peace and relief that I require at any time. It is also a time for Release, but we will get to that part of the practice a little later.

Let's break this information into simple sections that we can examine and digest, then understand how it applies to your survivorship.

WHY

Every person that engages and embraces meditation has their own reasons for doing so, but in the context of this book, let's just consider why silence and meditation would be such a good practice for us as survivors. Our minds, bodies and spirits have—and maybe still are—taking such a tremendous and stressful daily impact as a result of losing a loved one, compounded by the fact that the death was the result of suicide. How to cope with suicide is almost impossible to calculate, and the degree it affects our human vessel is nearly immeasurable. The grief, the anger, the confusion, sleeplessness, flashbacks, depression, isolation, all takes the most unbelievable toll on the physical self. It can and often does make us sick; sick of body and sick of heart.

If depression is something that has entered your life since the event, I would hope that you have sought the advice and care of a physician and/or mental health professional. If you suspect that you are clinically depressed or have had your own thoughts of suicide—not uncommon to those of suicide loss—I would urge you to call a medical professional as early as possible. No-one but us knows how hard this all is. These seven tools that you are learning here, while they work well on their own, also work incredibly well in tandem with medical care and treatments of all types including professional psychotherapies and medications. Drugs to combat depression are on the rise in America. From 2005 to 2008, it was determined by the Center for Disease Control that as many as 11 percent of Americans, (1 in every 10 people) twelve years of age and older were on some type of antidepressant therapy including Tricyclics, MAO inhibitors, SSRIs, as well as several other categories of antidepressant medications. Antidepressants are the third most common prescription drug taken by Americans today. These drugs are good, we need them for various diagnoses and they save lives.

Having said that, let me offer that there are any number of adjunct therapies that will work with medications and will make a monumental difference in the wellbeing of the human body under duress. What pills can do for the body, silence, meditation and release can do for the mind and spirit. None of this is mutually exclusive – everything can work together, so why not give it the best shot we have toward full success? Trying to work through and comprehend your presence of mind regarding the death of someone so close to you cannot be wrapped up in just one chemical tablet. Talking with a professional about your fears and concerns helps to identify what you are struggling with the most and the therapies that would work best for you. We all need clarity on what to work on and what is holding us back. A professional counselor listens to you and you can listen to them as well; at the same time, how do *you* listen to *you*? The "you within" that has something to say, needs a voice and a release of thought and ideas, right? I often think that Drew listened to so much information from the outside—what to fear in the world according to the news media; what job would give him the best advantage; who to know to get ahead; even what to buy and wear that would put him in the best light—that he may have lost his own good advice. As smart as he was, when did he quiet that overactive mind of his and recognize that his inner self had powerful knowledge to offer for his wellbeing?

So the first step is accepting that there are any number of therapies and modalities that can give us strength and guidance every day, some of which are not necessarily high up on the scientific hit list. If you already do or are familiar with silent time, mindfulness or meditation, you have a leg up on why it could be important at this fragile juncture of your life. Consider every avenue to your healing and be open to its likely success.

WHEN

This is easy—whenever and wherever you can find the time and quiet location. Here is the harder part. Make sure you find the time and quiet location. If your schedule doesn't give you a break, then it should be your intention to give your schedule the break. The reality is that if you choose to use this tool as a healing source, you will find the time and the location and make it work.

I spoke with a dear friend of mine, actually Drew's best friend in the whole world, about how his Still-Mind meditation was coming along. He responded that he had recently meditated in his car waiting for a job interview. I asked him why he did that, and he responded that he wanted to create some balance before going through the interview which was likely to be grueling. I understood that perfectly. Perhaps his choice of locations wasn't the most ideal, but his reasons were spot on. A good rule of thumb is to be silent and meditative when you know you need it the most; and if necessary, on the spot. In working through healing of survivorship, it makes perfect sense to meditate whenever the stress of the body and mind is more predominant than your regular activity. The time you choose can be very personal. Perhaps first thing in the morning when you know you have to face the day, you can set the balance and tone that will help you cope with what is ahead of you. If you are struggling with sleep deprivation due to flashbacks or anxiety, maybe just before retiring for the night will give you the edge you need to sleep better. If you wake in the middle of it all, still-mind and deep breathing can get you right back to sleep. The idea is to turn off the outside stuff and listen to the beautiful language in your heart. Be still, and breathe.

WHERE

Sometime in the future you will be able to do meditation anywhere, but for now let's be reasonable and say that you should choose the location wisely. The key is to make it as much "yours" as possible. It can be a whole room or an area 4 ft. by 4 ft., as long as you set it up to be your ally in peace. This is not a spot to bring your cell or laptop – believe it or not, they are toxic and have no place in your Place. Use a chair, a rug, a flameless or flame candle, silence or guided meditation, crystals or favorite artifacts,

whatever. Consider this space your personal time-travel
location. Why so formal? Because it will encourage you
to use it and make it available at a moment's notice –
especially when you need it because of what is going on
around you and within you. Breathing goes hand-in-
hand with Silence/Meditation/and Release; therefore,
"when the goings-on are going-in," get to where you have
relief before it starts really hurting you.

Your bed is another great spot for the "Where." If
you have a lot of trouble with your sleep time, silence
and meditation before retiring for the night is a great
step toward resting the body for longer periods. Using
a guided meditation that puts you in relaxation mode is
excellent; just find one that is about 17-20 minutes long,
has a soothing voice and gives you breaks for contem-
plation. You may refer to the section in references for
some tried and true CDs that do that. I am a real prima
donna about guided meditations and you can trust the
ones that I have listed for you to try.

Silence plus DB is another perfect combination before sleep. The challenge here is that we often use this
time to go over and over the thoughts and decisions of
the day, ones that worked and ones that didn't, so do
consider the guided versions and save the silence for
other points in the day, especially when you are in your
quiet place. It will all work however you set it up, so be
patient with yourself and remember to practice.

If you are in a strange or new place and you need to quiet yourself, simply look around for a spot that will meet your needs even temporarily. Let someone know that you are taking some time for yourself and where you will be so that they can run interference or at the very least stop themselves from knocking on doors to locate you. Often when we are in situations where our progress toward healing is being challenged by specific conditions or conversations, Silence/Meditation is the answer to keeping it together. No apologies are required! Just do what you need to do to bring your balance back in place, the best way you can. I can remember moments that if one more person spoke to me, my chest would implode. Getting away for breathing and silence can be a lifesaver for your emotions and your anger. The more you are practicing it, the easier and quicker you can make it work for you under any circumstances and locations.

How

Now we are getting to the actual steps you can take to achieve Still-Mind through silence, mindfulness or other types of meditation. This is the place where I assure you that quieting your mind and turning your attention inward is not hard to do. It simply takes repetition, practice and understanding the principle of "quiet body, quiet mind, healing body." Remember our lawn sweeper guy earlier in this chapter? All he needed was an empty room and a chair to sit on. He didn't even want to use any kind of music or sound to assist in his meditation – quiet space was his only requirement. There are many good folks around with tools and opportunity to help you on this path, and if you prefer to take advantage of their skills and locations, by all means do so. You may wish to search out various meditation styles that vary somewhat from what I suggest, but know that you can find something that really works for you. Do remember that once you decide on *what* you want to do, make the time and effort to *do* it.

THE PRACTICE: MEDITATION/SILENCE

WHAT YOU NEED:
You may wish to have a principal focus, better known as a *focal point*. The purpose or use of a focal point is for something to become the central point of attention or interest within your visionary field if you are one to keep your eyes open. If you choose not to close your eyes during meditation, it is a place for your eyes to be, as opposed to scanning around and looking at everything else. It can be a small or flickering item placed in a spot

in front of you. It can also be a picture or brightly colored item on the wall. If you do not need a focal point, then you may wish to simply close your eyes and picture a focal point in your mind.

WHAT YOU DO:

1. Pick your time to meditate carefully. Allow for the fact that this time frame of 10 to 30 minutes is for you exclusively, and interruption is not to be expected in any way. Pave the way for this requirement to be met on the part of all others if need be.

2. Pick your location. A room, a separate or secluded area is best. Decide where and on what you will sit, lie down or recline. Make sure the accommodations are comfortable and meet your physical needs completely or as close to completely as possible. Assemble any items that will assist you in being relaxed and without pressure on your body – pillows, head rest, rolled towel, etc.

3. Remove and safely store—away from your meditation area—any electronic or communication devices that will divert your attention from going

within. You may want to let someone else know your intentions about not being disturbed or interrupted and let them be your gatekeeper for the period of time that you require.

4. If you are using a guided meditation – one that requires headphones, CD player – make sure you assemble that device for your meditation. This would be the same if you prefer to have Zen or soft meditation music accompany your journey. If you decide to have no auditory assistance, simply prepare the area as stated above.

5. Create a focal point that may initially assist you on your meditation. It can be a colorful point on the wall, a crystal, or a flameless or real candle on a table in front of you. An indoor waterfall or water sounds feature is also acceptable and very useful. If no focal point is needed, simply focus with eyes open on a distant point or close your eyes gently against the light.

6. Consciously soften your muscles: neck and shoulders, especially. Relax your arms, wrists, hands and your belly – you have no one to impress so let your tummy relax completely. Tighten and release the muscles in your thighs and lower legs. Rotate and relax your ankles and feet. Feel these muscles making full contact with whatever

they are resting on. Flatten and soften yourself against the floor or chair supports.

7. Always begin with three deep breaths prior to clearing your mind. For a reminder on breathing technique, refer to the section on how to involve DB completely and with correct technique.

8. Through your focal point or with eyes closed, create a blank slate or dark gray-colored area behind your eyes. Rest your inner vision here without seeing anything in particular.

9. If something substantial intrudes that has nothing whatsoever to do with quiet mind, and it involves your current day, decision making, or anxiousness, gently send it over to the side away from your blank slate and tell "it" you will manage whatever it is later. Allow your blank slate to return to your inner vision. Do this as often as necessary and each time it intrudes. Be patient, your mind will get the message eventually and your blank slate will stay longer and longer.

10. Colors may spontaneously move around in your slate space. Allow them to move freely without putting any understanding to them. Do not judge their shapes, do not control their movement. They are there to soften your meditation.

Embrace the color and note how it makes you feel.

11. Focus on normal breathing and listen to the air going in and out of your nose and mouth. Select a word to accompany the exhale, such as Love or Peace, Om or God. Draw the word out gently, using the entire exhale. Create a rhythm of in and out with your mantra word if you wish. If your mind is trying to be busy, it will be your breathing focus that makes that go away. If you think about how you are breathing and what it feels like, you cannot think about other stuff.

12. Breathing and still mind is all you are shooting for. Maintain the rhythm and peace. When you feel soft and relaxed, you will know when you are ready to "come back." It will amaze you how much time has passed.

13. Expect that you may also "hear" some information or message at some point in your meditation practice. It will be very different from the chatter or angst that is usually clogging our thinking. It will be positive, answer a question you have asked, or it will give you a loving emotion. You needn't ask for it or wish for it – simply let it come when you are in a relaxed state.

14. When your meditation is concluding, return to the three deep breaths that you started with at the onset. Consciously feel your extremities, normalize your breathing and open your eyes when you are ready.

15. Say a sincere "thank you" to your inner self for the quiet journey you have just taken. Gratitude should always be expressed for the positive experience you witness whenever you meditate. Even if the meditation was not as easy or as successful as you'd hoped, by giving your appreciation to yourself, you set your mind up for the success of next time. It's all good.

16. Stretch and put your arms straight up towards the ceiling in an open stance, embracing the greatness around you.

THE PRACTICE: MINDFULNESS

1. Remember the difference between silence meditation and mindfulness meditation. Mindfulness is using your entire sensing systems to give you an in-the-moment experience and healing.

2. As in all meditations, begin your practice by using your deep breathing methods to calm your body and mind.

3. Choose the location for being mindful. This can be anywhere you wish, indoors or outdoors. As in the other meditation preparations, you should assure yourself, and perhaps others, that an interruption is not desired.

4. Mindfulness can be done with eyes open or closed, but some portion of your time within it would sincerely benefit by being mindful visually. It assists the overall meditation and the healing encounter.

5. Use your entire body to manifest the meditation through total awareness. Skin sensations, muscle alignment, skeletal condition, sound, color, temperature and pressure are allies to being aware.

6. As with other meditation, unhealthy thoughts and concerns are not wanted here and should be gently laid aside for determination later. Lovely, subtle, gentle observations that produce positive reflections are allowed and even desired. Examples would be: how blue that bird is and how incredibly beautiful its song is affecting me; I am amazed at the softness of the soil that is under my bare feet; at the horizon the water and the sky seem to blend into one so well I can't seem to tell the difference. Each one of these examples can produce a mindfulness exercise of its own.

7. Mindfulness can be done doing one simple task or fifteen minutes of observation at some location. (I kindly refer you to the reference section for a very nice blog by Alfred James on basic mindfulness exercises that will give you help on getting started.)

Release

(Part II)

"Secrecy involves a tension which, at the
moment of revelation, finds its release."

— GEORG SIMMEL

PERHAPS YOU ARE WONDERING ABOUT the quote at the beginning of this section. Secrecy – really? The facts are
that the things and memories that reside in our subconscious mind are quite secret. We don't bring them out
easily and generally can't get them to stir without some
kind of help to do so. These secrets just sort of sit there,
often for a very long time, years even. At the time they

occur, we attach an emotion to them, and we seldom predict when the effects of their existence deep within will make themselves known again. If the secret is not one that we would consider very pretty or acceptable, we probably chose to leave it alone at all costs, and want to forget it even has residence in there.

Practicing meditation calms the mind, body and spirit. That is true, but it also does a little stirring and fermenting of the hidden emotional secrets we have suppressed. This shouldn't be a shock to anyone, but it often feels that way when your meditation suddenly makes you feel angry, restless or unhappy. Your inner being knows these emotions need to surface, but your outer being can be quite surprised and confused by it. This is Release just waiting to happen. It's a good thing, actually, a very good thing.

The hidden issues that are associated with emotion want to be healed, and meditation allows for you to re-experience, observe and let go of what you no longer need. If we don't make time and opportunity to release what is not healthy, it will discover another way to annoy us, or worse, hurt us. Generally, that manifests as something physical or mental. This old junk isn't doing you and your body any good anyway, so there is virtually no reason to hold on to it. In order to move more smoothly through the process of Release, my good advice is, to let it come before you let it go. Easy to say when you find it a bit uncomfortable to experience: you can sometimes feel physical changes such as headaches, stomach issues, sleeplessness and tension. Emotional conditions arise as well similar to sadness, crying inexplicably or feeling anger. But wait, isn't meditation supposed to help us with this stuff? Yes, and that is exactly what you are doing, even when you may experience some emotional and physical responses. Meditation is giving you the path by which it can all be dealt with for the last time. Obviously, we didn't handle it that well in the first place. Now is the time to not resist, but to stand to the side and observe dispassionately what is taking place. It feels like a tall order, but it is healing beyond description. As survivors, this is a prescription for success.

Release is letting go of that which does not produce positive energy for you any longer. Releasing can be spontaneous or consciously done. When it is spontaneous, your inner emotional state of mind just does it for you. It knows that you need to release and you can feel it happen in your body or heart. In the instance of spontaneous, it is almost shocking since you really didn't know it was coming. Sometimes you actually don't know it has come and gone – you simply feel better or great. Some people will state that it feels like a huge weight has just been lifted off of their shoulders and mind. Other folks may feel purged and feather-light. You have experienced that, we all have. It's generally un-named, but appreciated.

When you release consciously, you have identified an emotional turmoil, bad feeling or event that is blocking you and you simply *Let It Go*. Examples of this might be a long-associated painful relationship that has plagued you, parental blame, personal blame, things you have done that you regret, hate issues, food issues, money worries and others. State it out loud to yourself – "I release this (thing), including all of the energies and feelings that are associated with it!" At the end of your meditation, before you say thank you, see this block (with your inner eye) as being no longer in your secret hoard of buried stuff. Set an intention that you will no longer require the need to hold onto whatever it is. Visualize your body free of the negative energy. It is not hard to release, but you have to want to and then believe it gone.

There are so many times as survivors we hold onto guilt concerning the sudden death of our loved one. By releasing the guilt we unjustly carry with us at the conclusion of a meditation, we have just given ourselves the gift of better health. We do not own any guilt, so why not release what we don't own? Like intention, like deep breathing, release just gets better and better every time we practice it.

EXPOSURE THERAPY

Exposure therapy is a very specific type of cognitive-behavioral technique that can be used in the treatment of post-traumatic stress disorder (PTSD) and phobias such as panic disorders.

The intent of Exposure Therapy is to help the patient face the paralyzing fear in the trauma, expose them within very specific guidelines and steps, and to assist them in safely coping for the future around this fearful blockage. The techniques used during the treatments are carefully conducted by a licensed or certified individual, allowing the client to learn the exercises of relaxation and imagery, so as not to re-traumatize. A therapist works with the client to determine which method is best suited for their specific fear or phobia.

According to the American Psychological Association, within which is the Society of Clinical Psychology, Exposure Therapy can be an effective treatment to help people confront their worst fears. [3] Individuals experiencing long-term grief have a tendency to avoid activities, situations, objects and places associated with the grief itself. As survivors of suicide loss, we either are aware of or can imagine much of what would be our greatest fear. With Exposure Therapy a psychologist will create a safe environment where they can gradually expose the client to the things or situations that traumatized them in the first place. The therapy is complex and tailored to the client's current mental status and the extension of the fear they have been facing. There are many pathways to choose in conducting the therapy appropriately.

Important to note: *To avoid unwanted outcomes, this therapy should always be conducted with a therapist who is trained and experienced in all areas of the treatment, and the exercises to prevent the client from being re-traumatized. This is simply good medicine.*

A PERSONAL STORY

(Dealing with the dreaded location - I did this on my own and I don't recommend you do it.)

As I slowly conquered many of the hardships and challenges that a survivor is faced with, there was one struggle that would nearly paralyze me every time – that was driving near "the location," seeing a building that was even similar in shape or seeing the name of the town where Drew chose to end his life. I am a rational person and my physical response during these trips was nothing like I had ever encountered in my life. In the end, I was literally incapacitated with fear. I would sweat, my stomach would turn and I would weep with anxiety. I knew I needed to decide if this situation would forever follow me and keep me from enjoying any travel to anywhere ever again, let alone close to home.

At that time, I was not under the guidance or care of anyone professional, with the exception of my primary care physician. She had asked me on several occasions if I wanted to be referred to a therapist. At this point I had repeatedly declined, and thinking back, I seemed to be flying by the seat of my pants most of the time. In my experience, nurses are pretty stubborn that way. In the end, I decided it would help me to encounter my fear head-on. Perhaps I was not making the best decision without consulting a psychotherapist or counselor, but right or wrong, I took things into my own hands. Looking back on my decision to confront, I realize now how close my activity—obviously by angelic guidance or by accident—modeled the Exposure Therapy described in my research. My guardian angels were with me on this trip. Being a spiritual person I often work with symbolic items and ceremonies in my energy work, so I planned my visit to the location, using the props that help me, but most importantly setting my Intention.

My intention was: I will see this location as simply a build-ing. I will release my fear and sadness to this place for all time. It was not the cause of Drew's distress— it was simply a space choice that he made.

I selected early morning, thinking there would be no one around and I could deal with my mission quietly and privately. Fortunately, that didn't happen. I found myself parking in the same spot that Drew had parked, but didn't realize it because there were so many other cars there already. Was that coincidence? I think not. My props were candles, ceremonial tobacco (bear with me here), and a container for sand to bring back home.

I began my encounter with deep breathing as I always do when facing fear or emotional challenge. Then I began walking through all the areas of the building that I walked on that fateful day. At each stop, I dropped some tobacco and released the spot of any responsibility, anger or fear. I released the floor, walls, ceilings and declared them simple space. I moved on to stairwells, hallways, doorways and furniture. I continued until I had walked in all the same footsteps as I had three and one-half years ago. A huge weight was slowly but effectively lifting off my shoulders with each moment and step I moved through. I saw this building for what it was – a building with walls, windows and physical structure, nothing more. It held no mystery, no calling for justice, and no evil intent.

When I was finished with my releasing journey inside, and as I exited the outer doors, I stomped my feet on the pavement and told myself, "I am done with fear here!" I lit some candles on the beach and smiled as the sun warmed my skin. I was doing mindfulness and being in the now moment, clearly. Everywhere I looked were dozens of people walking and enjoying the early morning sun, water and sand with their dogs and their friends and their loved ones. I believed with all my heart that they had come specifically to join me in my Intention, having no idea why they had made the decision to come to this particular beach, at this hour. In turn, each person said hello to me as I stood there. In my heart I knew they had been called in some way to do a remarkable service at that very moment. It was emotionally moving to think how "un-alone" I was. I smiled and picked up a stone that was heart shaped, with two more heart images within it. Wow, where did that come from? Every time I beach-walk I search for heart stones and never, ever find any; here was one stone with three hearts on it! As I threw it into the water, I said my intention with surety one more time. It may not be the beach I choose first as a swimming hole, but I no longer fear it or hate it. I was at peace with this place.

I give you my experience here, not because it was necessarily the correct way to do it, but it signifies the power of release. Without knowing it, I seemed to be using some sequence work that is used in Exposure Therapy without the benefit of a trained individual to help me through it. But I used my relaxation techniques of deep breathing and mindfulness to provide me with permanent elimination of the severe trigger that I was always going to be subject to if I didn't do something about it. I found gratitude in the people that were called to be with me, without them even knowing what incredible gifts they had to donate. I was filled with abundance of sun, amazing sea breezes, and the refreshing, rebirthing waters in my Soul.

To you my readers, I would recommend always checking with your medical and social practitioners for guidance on how it may affect you and what they would suggest for your good care. My point is that my phobia of the location was personal to me and represented a fear that stopped me from moving forward in a healthy way. If I didn't deal with it, I was bound to bury it and that can never be a good thing. Our experiences are all different, our "locations" each have an effect; one fix is not good for all.

This was my fix and it brought me forward to a healing I never knew could happen.

God was certainly watching over me, and somehow I feel I only came out of it intact because He was watching! Being re-traumatized was not something I would have wanted to happen.

The Practice: Release

The purpose of this exercise is to practice letting go of energy, information, or emotional baggage that no longer serves to help or heal you, and actually blocks you from progress. Releasing requires no explanations or apologies to yourself or anyone else. Like that famous shoe company... Just Do It!

WHAT YOU NEED:

1. A few seconds of uninterrupted thought.

WHAT YOU DO:

1. Identify the useless, toxic or emotional trigger that needs to be let go. It may arise spontaneously or you might call upon it because you recognize its venom through conscious thought.
2. Give it your full attention, describe it clearly and visualize what it looks like. "See" it in its full context as if you were standing off to the side of "you." State out loud or silently, "I release this thought, feeling, condition or behavior to the Universe. I no longer need to hold it."
3. You can mentally or physically stomp your feet, brush your hands, or smile to yourself. Say goodbye to IT and thank you to yourself.

Examples of some simple releases:

* Guilty thoughts of what you might have done today, but didn't get accomplished. Example: "I release the need to feel always busy and doing, I give myself permission to spend quality time with and for me."

* Being angry with a family member for saying something hurtful. Example: "I release my anger at this person, now. Whatever is being directed toward me does not belong to me – it belongs to them. They cannot hurt me if I don't let them."

* Taking a day off to accomplish something important to you, instead of driving someone else to an appointment. Example: "I release the guilt about saying 'no' whenever I feel the need to."

* Asking for help when you think you should be doing it yourself without help. Example: "I release my fear of losing independence. I will recognize and accept when help would do me such good."

* Moving emotionally away from a friend or acquaintance because they make you unhappy or uncomfortable. Example: "I release my fear of being alone or without friends. I am confident of my ability to seek out companionship that is healthy and joyful, whenever I want."

❀ Identifying with an item, piece of clothing, furniture, store, food, photo, room or other thing that makes you feel sad or uncomfortable, brings unwelcome memories or instills fear. Example: "I release my fear of any item or place that makes me unhappy or upset. I choose to go to those places or touch only those things that I am comfortable with. I will provide no explanations to anyone but myself for what I do or think."

RELEASING EVERYONE'S REACTIONS

It is worth mentioning the emotional and memory "blanks" that can occur in your timeline or the timelines of others. What do I mean by blanks? Have you ever been involved in an auto accident or injury, or witnessed some event that moved like lightning speed, and then tried to identify or remember all the frames of it minute by minute to someone else? Often the first words out of your mouth are, "It happened so fast – I'm not sure I can recall the correct sequence of events accurately."

In extreme distress, remembering detail and losing focus *or* keeping focus and losing detail can happen. Your mind will try to find any way to protect you even to the point of losing an entire day. One of the most important things to understand is to never blame yourself for what you remember or don't remember. This is a brain on overload—incomprehensible data at the time of greatest stress. I still have lost time slots from the days and weeks after losing Drew, and while I am certain it is all recorded in my brain somewhere, recalling much of it accurately seems out of reach. We will all handle this differently. Simply forgiving ourselves and others for when this happens is the best course of action – release the need for clarification and detail. Your body is doing what it needs to do to protect you, sometimes permanently, from what is too painful to handle now. If the details return to you at some future time, process them with gentleness and patience, talk them over with someone, a counselor or trusted friend, then release them using the steps that have been discussed previously. Just go with what works for you, and never consider that you are not responding correctly to any situation that you find yourself in or blindsided by.

CHAPTER 6

Allowing and Zero Judgment

"The Master acts on what he feels not what he
sees, so (he) allows things to come and go."

— LAO TZU, THE TAO TE CHING, VERSE 12

WHEN WE ALLOW WE ARE recognizing, through deliberate
action and understanding, everyone's given right to have
a thought, opinion or personal declaration. Done perfectly, this process must include Zero Judgment, in which
we successfully avoid forming an opinion or conclusion
regarding the circumstances presented to us. Neither
"We" nor "They" should ever feel the need to move from

our own basis of belief in order to keep the relationship in balance. We should conduct our different approaches to something, with respect and curiosity – give room to learn, grow and yet choose to stay put without recrimination or consequences.

Good grief, how often do we do that? Most of us have a hundred opinions about the most miniscule topics, and we never seem to hesitate in telling the world how we feel about it. This paves the way for standing in judgment of another person, simply because their thoughts and ideas do not match up with our own. Here are some simple examples. Just put little quotes around each one of these – you will recognize your own voice, I promise.

- Here's what you do.
- Let me tell you just what to do.
- There is a much better way to do this.
- You never did understand about …
- I can't believe you voted for him/her! What were you thinking?
- Did you see that? Awful, atrocious, stupid, ugly, ridiculous, tacky, too small, too big…
- I have never seen anything so dumb in my whole life!
- That's not how I would have handled *that* situation.

- I will not tolerate your (their) attitude.
- Your religion, (politics, parenting, fashion) is not the best, you must know it!
- The way they are fixing this is all wrong.
- My way or the highway, friend.

In general, many of us have been raised to have some sort of an opinion or at least be able to form one pretty quickly. Our family life, nationality, ethics and mores usually have a strong hand and influence on how we do this. We frequently attribute this ability to how intelligent, worldly, busy and savvy we are – sometimes it's a simple matter of showing how much backbone we think we should have. We are nothing if not gifted in the ways of life, and trying to come out on top.

Allowing is a tough stretch for many, if not most. Here's the thing, even if we don't say our opinion, we are thinking it. Dear reader, in my experience, there is no difference. Our actions will always reflect what we really believe and want you to believe in in exactly the same way. Winning an argument or discussion makes me look good, and always brings more companions to my side of the fence. When I say I allow, but harbor a secretive belief opposite to that, I am not allowing at all. I am condemning you quietly instead. If what I think is what I manifest, it will come out in the end, somewhere.

How does this work for or against us as survivors? You have the opportunity to allow with no apologies or excuses, and this is an extremely important tool for you now and for always. Your life as a survivor is very complex. You are often in the middle of people who are there to support you or wish to support you, but the topic of suicide is not one that they are comfortable with. Hell, you're not comfortable with it! It is nearly impossible to predict how any conversations are going to emerge that don't bring some type of uncomfortable issues right along with them. Since everyone has a form of baggage associated with life in general, the likelihood of being drawn into any scenario that is of a polarizing nature is high. Everyone has an opinion. Everyone has gossip. Everyone can't wait to share their opinion or their gossip with someone else; basically it comes down to hauling stinky bags of judicial garbage around and asking anyone and everyone to smell it.

In the wake of the suicide you might hear such statements as: the fire and rescue were slow; someone made mistakes; the doctors were inadequate; you need to bring a lawsuit; things would have turned out differently *if*; don't share or tell the family what you know... the list of possibilities is virtually endless. You will most sincerely be on the receiving end of this type of interaction at multiple times.

So much of our life after suicide requires choices and change, and frankly we can lose patience with a lot of it. I don't know about you, but I never was one to embrace change well, unless it involved only moving my furniture around. Everything else had to stay the course if I was going to keep order. Because I was the "easy-going" one in my family, I found myself being the fence sitter. You know what I mean, go along to get along. I somehow became the peace-keeper and the person that everyone came to, to gain points for their side. People like me were identified as the ones who have ears everyone wants to bend.

When survivorship was forced upon me, I lost my tolerance for all of that "go along to get along" crap—overnight. If I was going to be able to keep my head above water in any way, I needed to get my beliefs underfoot and keep them there, since everything else was shifting badly. I learned Allowing first, even before non-judgment, but it was the right track to follow. How do you stay balanced without falling into fear, anger or guilt? What can you do to avoid being pulled into someone else's collusion, especially if it hurts you in some way? You allow.

There are two types of Allowing. One type is when you allow for *someone else,* and the other concerns allowing for *yourself.*

Allowing for someone else

In the long run, you need to exercise tools that will help you state your feelings, speak your truth, and make no excuses. None are needed anyway. *With allowing, you are never pulled or pushed into any position that is not yours or does not suit you, unless you let it.* The second part of allowing someone else must include non-judgment of their expression to you. If you allow it, you need to avoid judging it, simply because you don't need to embrace it. It belongs to them, so why bother christening it right or wrong?

For the purposes of clarity and further understanding of the practice of Allowing for someone else, I will discuss two examples. First I will give the scenario, and then I will present the use of Allowing on just one way to mentally and emotionally deal with the positive outcome. One example does not concern a survivor of suicide loss, but you will be able to see how it could. What these examples will provide are clear situations that are applicable for anyone trying to comprehend true Allowing.

Example A:

You are in the post office parking lot and a car pulls in the space next to you. The driver of this vehicle opens the driver side and thoughtlessly bangs their car door right into yours. When the driver emerges, you are tempted to say something really stinging about what they just did. You notice that their car is very old and somewhat dinged already. The driver looks agitated and her clothing and hair is disheveled. Her eyes are red and maybe she doesn't appear in a very good mood or emotionally put together. Now maybe your vehicle isn't the most beautiful, but it's yours and you care about it. Do you raise your voice, and tell her that she is thoughtless and uncaring about other people's precious belongings? Do you say nothing and just fume?

The Allowing:
What if this woman has just come from the hospital where a family member is in a critical condition? She hasn't slept in two days keeping vigil at the bedside, she hasn't changed her clothes or brushed her hair, and she has little cash to help her get by in any situation, including gas for her old car. At this moment she is in a stressful hurry because if the mail doesn't get out this very minute, her bills will be past due. She's on the brink.

How would any of us know her circumstances? How can we possibly comprehend her stress, her fears, her anger at what life is bringing to her family right now? She probably doesn't even see you or your car door; she is simply trying to survive the day. Her world is crashing down around her head… or, she is thoughtless and just wants to get on to her next task and doesn't care anything about you and your vehicle – it's just the way she is every single day of the year. We are not in a position to know that, either.

By allowing the possibility that you can seldom, if ever, really know what is happening with another human being who is demonstrating behaviors you do not care for – it is kind and wise to refrain from retaliation. Notice, I said retaliation. Her situation could be your situation. As the recipient of unwanted behavior, as in this example, it does not mean you are giving up your belief that we should always be respectful of other people's property. It does not mean that you are condoning poor and disrespectful behavior on the part of others. It does mean that perhaps there is something that you don't know, and it is wise to avoid a judgment of the circumstances. In reality, the loss of your loved one from tragic circumstances may have made you act in ways that others considered unacceptable, and they witnessed something they did not understand. I still cannot remember how I responded to many conversations, tasks, questions and circumstances. How many of them made me look and/or act as our woman at the post office? Some of my friends and family probably had difficulty allowing at the time towards me, but that doesn't mean we can't learn how.

EXAMPLE B:

You are in the presence of a friend or a family member, and they can't wait to discuss a very polarizing situation with you regarding the way to handle some legal issues connected with your loss. It may be a decision you have been wrestling with since it first came to your attention, and this person is convinced that they can help you with the solution to this problem you face. Undoubtedly they have an opinion – a strong one. You can see it coming. What they really want is for you to listen to their idea and to act accordingly on their expert advice. They bring their story and preface it with all the information you will need to climb right over to their side of the fence, even though they are not in any way responsible for the outcome. You know from the past that the more you resist, the more they push; and you further know, that if you don't do as they have suggested, they will be very unhappy with you. Maybe more than one person will be unhappy.

THE ALLOWING:

In this case you are giving your acquaintance the opportunity to have their say about their understanding of the situation. If you listen and decide that you are not in agreement or have sincere doubts about the reason they are attempting to get your agreement, you have no need to capitulate. That is how we lose our own footing and self-esteem – we get by through going along, creating enormous pools of stress. You can allow them to feel and believe the way they do without climbing over the fence simply to sustain a relationship. You allow yourself to remain within a comfort zone consistent with your own belief and decision-making process; at the same time you allow that someone's ideas or solutions, while respected, are not necessarily going to work for you. We do not have to participate in a polarizing jaunt. We thank them for their input, and make the best decision for ourselves and our circumstances – no explanations required.

ALLOWING FOR YOURSELF

In this type of allowing, you are giving yourself the benefit of grace in the face of unexpected or questionable thoughts and behavior of your own. Did you not respond or handle something very well? Did you get angry, beat yourself up a bit, regret an outcome you couldn't see coming, manage to screw up miserably because your sadness was just overwhelming? This is the place where you say, "Ah well, I will just forgive me for that – I will do better next time, because now I know..." This allowing is just as important as allowing someone else – maybe more. You are the most important person in the world, and you are learning how to navigate through this very difficult journey toward healing. You want to do it right all the time, but you just can't when the training sessions are slam dunk blind-siders. Do cut yourself even more slack than you would others. You have never experienced this in your wildest nightmares, and you are doing the very best you can. Again, there is the component of non-judgment here, only this time, you avoid judging yourself as someone who didn't measure up. To do that would be to undo all that you have just allowed on your own behalf. Figure out what you might do differently if you want, but more importantly, love yourself and move on to the next task.

EXAMPLE A:

When your loved one took their own life, they left an incredible amount of untended things behind; from banking accounts and invoices to a home or rental in complete disarray. Your first reaction is anger and mental distress for needing to manage it all, and then the next reaction is a total wash of guilt for even complaining. Isn't this clean up situation somewhat negligible when compared to having your loved one gone from you permanently? You hate yourself for being angry about "stuff" and you would give anything to have them back with you again.

THE ALLOWING:

In this scenario it is yourself that you are allowing for. You are allowing your reactions to what you are experiencing. This is allowing for you and by you. It is completely understandable that your initial reaction is anger and guilt. Just as we find it impossible to comprehend what others are going through in any given situation, we need to be gentle on ourselves for what we are going through. In this example we are facing a huge task that is laden with overtones of loss and tragedy. We allow that guilt is a rapid second response to pain and grief, and we give ourselves permission to accept that as such. We are being human in a human vessel. Esther Hicks, channeling Abraham, says it best in *The Law of Attraction*. "True allowing is maintaining your own balance, your own joy, no matter what they (others) are doing." As survivors, we work so much harder than many others toward maintaining balance, trying to keep our heads above the water line, when so much is pushing us down. By using your emotional responses as a meter of what is going on inside you, you can judge whether you are in a good thinking place or in a not-so-good thinking place, but please don't stand in judgment of how it was handled. Allow that not-so-good thinking places are just another way of learning the navigation of this strange and bumpy path we have been—regretfully—assigned to follow.

EXAMPLE B:

I have dear friends and family who have been standing close at hand since the news of my loss. Their sympathy and kindness has been one of the most sustaining gifts I could ever ask for under such frightening circumstances when I feel so lost. But one dear friend that I have known most of my life has virtually abandoned me in my time of need. She does not call or respond to my communications and messages; she never even bothered to send a card of comfort. There are virtual strangers who have been giving their time and energy to make my days easier, but where is one of the most important people in my life? I am angry and devastated by this. I think she should simply stay away from me forever and make a vow to forget we ever had a relationship. I am better off without this individual in my life. Now, several months after my loss, I am wondering what I have truly lost in the aftermath of everything. Perhaps I did something to offend or omitted a loving connection somehow. Was it me?

THE ALLOWING:

This is the opportunity for you to participate in both types of allowing. First, allow that there is nothing that you could or should have done to maintain a friendship on your own. It will always require two people to form a bond that stands through adversity; one individual is not enough to keep it going. Give yourself the grace that under the worst of the fire, you were trying to survive, and in many ways still are. Your response to her lack of connection must not induce guilt on your heart. Allow that all is well in whatever you do or think. When you manage compassion for your responses, you avoid placing judgment on both of you. Her problem is not your problem.

Secondly, allow that your friend was incapable of comprehending or accepting the depths of emotion that surrounded you during and after this event. It was easier to stay away and do nothing than cope with such tragedy inadequately. Perhaps she never did possess the skillset to be compassionate and supportive, and never will. That will be her journey, not yours.

A SURVIVORS' GREATEST QUESTION

Why did they do it? So how can allowing help you with that terrible—and most asked—least answered question? I have dared to make the statement that I thought Drew, following his death, was one of the bravest people I ever knew. How can I say that? Why would I say that? Perhaps you have thought the same thing, or conversely, you felt that your loved one was weak and did a cowardly act in checking out of life instead of figuring it out. Let me attempt to explain my thoughts about this and see how it resonates with you, but more importantly, how the understanding of Allowing helps you.

When I think of all of the years Drew suffered from panic attacks and we never knew he had them, it boggles my mind that he could fly so low under the radar while we were clueless. Talk about camouflage! This to me is amazing that he could appear to be fully in control on the outside, engage with others as if there was nothing wrong, be an expert in his field of endeavor, brilliant in the creativity required for his profession, love his children with his entire being, and be silently and slowly imploding. I also say brave because, in his mind I can only imagine that he felt suicide meant saving his family from himself, saving the world from himself, and saving himself from himself. Perhaps he could no longer keep up the pretense. I also say brave because Drew, like most victims of suicide, thought he was only involving himself. I suspect they truly believe that they are taking no-one with them and thus sparing the world of their fear, their anger and depressive acts. When he died as he did, people looked around at each other and formed the words...*what?* How is this possible? Who knew? I don't get it!

A young man who had attempted suicide twice in his life confided to me during my research, "We are con men, the best in the business. You will not know that we are in crisis and chaos. We will fool you every time." How much like Drew this sounds. In my heart of hearts I am hoping this gentleman has found his peace and does not ever achieve what he has tried twice before. But what about his point? If what he states is true, and given my firsthand knowledge regarding my own son, how then are we, as individuals so close to the primary behaviors of our loved ones, in a position to know what is going on underneath this seemingly fine exterior? What is this incredible ability to hide the internal destruction in plain sight? How do they do it? And for those victims that couldn't and didn't hide everything they were experiencing, what we must assume is that they were tamping down a boatload of pain, even while some of their fearful and depressive behaviors were spilling over.

Isn't that brave? It is to me.

To answer the question of why they did it requires a crystal ball, premonitions and sacred clues we just don't have access to. Our loved one had their one mind and their one body to live in. Even if they resided in the same house with us, we could never know how they perceived their world and their relationship to it. Seeking the answers to why suicide was the only answer for them is like looking for one specific grain of sand on the beach. These would-of, should-of, could-of queries to our brain would drive us all to the brink. So we need to try to stop doing that, beginning now.

Here is what we do instead: We *allow* that all decisions made surrounding the suicide of a loved one are owned by only one person – the deceased. And let's *allow* that the rights to those decisions, no matter how much we hate it, are granted to them from birth.

By allowing, we are finding a way to let go of the lack of control we never had in the first place, and let go of *our* feelings of responsibility over *their* decision. By allowing in this way, we recognize that the decision was made without our consultation or prior knowledge; so instead we stretch the very limits of what our emotions can do and we send healing love to our heart and to their heart as well. This is the epitome of zero-judgment. Just as in the definition of allow at the beginning of this chapter; I will let have; I will grant as one's right; I will admit, acknowledge, and concede, that Drew and all other victims made their decision and none of us helped them with it. They chose their road, and we love them for doing the best they could with what they had.

Between the interconnections of our immediate families, the news media, friends and neighbors, our religious affiliations and the medical community – we have an immense list of opportunities to allow and avoid judgment. The important question for you is where do you stand in your emotional adjustment? If you guide your emotions on the beliefs and judgments of everyone else, you will never be able to find your way to peace.

You will be living the thoughts and opinions of the rest of the world, and then requiring yourself to compensate for that.

IN THE AFTERMATH OF SUICIDE THERE ARE LOSSES FROM THE LOSS

People you thought as close friends and family that have always been in your circle suddenly abandon you. Their anger and issues surface at a time when you need their support the most. *Their* need to cope with the circumstances of this tragedy takes on a life of its own and involves you in ways you never thought possible. *If they cannot find their way to be at your side in the supportive gestures you absolutely require, it may be time to let them go, even if it is just for now.* In time they may come around in their personal healing, but until they do, they are on their own. You cannot fix them any more than you could fix your loved one.

A PERSONAL STORY

In the two days following Drew's death, I spent some hurried phone calls with my sister regarding the tragedy and next steps. She was the second person I spoke to on that day of discovery. She is the only immediate family member I have left, and her presence was going to be something I would need in the days and weeks to follow. By the second phone conversation, I had become aware of a clipped tone in her voice that bordered on rudeness. Where was this coming from? At first I simply thought I was imagining something that really didn't exist, but each succeeding exchange sounded worse than the last. By the time they arrived to my town late in the evening, all bets seemed to be off. She wouldn't stay at my house, wouldn't listen to any instructions about the memorial, and ultimately would not hug me or speak to me. She left the next day without attending any other functions of the funeral. How can it be that my sibling stops talking to me and will have nothing more to do with my life? This is not possible! Have I done something, anything, to warrant this behavior? I am left alone to bear up under new losses that are heaped directly on top of the worst loss in human existence. I am being blamed, accused, and I am totally blindsided. I wish to heaven this wasn't happening and I have NO idea what to do to fix it. Why am I in a position of dealing with someone else's reactions as well as my own? I don't know how to make this right – my world is in chaos!

I engage allowing and do my best not to engage in judging.

I cannot change what my sibling thinks and feels about my loss or me.

I cannot control how they grieve and what it will take to make them okay ever again.

That is her issue, and my recourse is to step away from "fixing it" and simply let go of the anger and blame and lack of forgiveness aimed at me. With allowing, my sister is entitled to think and do anything she may wish, but it will not be my concern to feed into it or feed on it. Instead I send her love, not solutions. I back away from what does not belong to me and allow her to deal with all of it on her own. I hope she can someday soon. It is worth repeating the channeled voice of Abraham through Esther Hicks. *Allowing is maintaining your own balance, no matter what others are doing.* I want to tell you what a relief it is when you let them go. This does not mean that you have to step in and fix and save. It does not mean that you no longer care about them or have stopped loving them. It means just what I said – *let them go.* Will they come back to you some day? Maybe. Maybe not. This is one of the hardest "allowing" there is, especially as in my case with the only immediate family member I have left in the whole world. The pain and anguish of trying to hold on to them and understand and make it right is horrible. But the relief from trying to figure it out is removed from your shoulders when you allow them to move away from your personal space – sometimes permanently.

You will heal better, faster, when you allow. I will not tell you this is easy, especially when your friends and other family members ask if you have contacted, written, cajoled, cried, begged...need I go on? Look at those who would push you in that direction endlessly and state with confidence, you are allowing these individuals to leave with grace. In my case, continued connection with my sister was toxic. I could not pour acid on an already open wound, so I allowed her to travel the journey without me. The door in my heart will always be open to receive in the future, but the door to my life as I exist from day to day is secure.

The support—or withdrawal of it—can also come from friends and the community at large. You really learn who your support systems are during times such as this. When I asked my dearest and closest to simply be by my side and say nothing that is exactly what they provided. No questions, just a hand at my back and an arm around my shoulder. If I was hearing too many inquiries, I allowed myself to back away from those individuals without providing the answers – that was my right of passage. Anyone who really loved me, understood perfectly. Having the strength to do that means you are taking charge, using your Intentions and progressing in a way that heals you. This is the practice that can and should be embraced for life, not just as the tool at the onset of grief. It does not matter whether your grief began four weeks ago or fourteen years ago.

A victim's final letter or note

Perhaps there was a final note left behind, but more than likely there was not. According to statistics, only 34 percent of victims leave behind a suicide letter of any kind. If there is a note written by the victim, it is likely to shed little, if any, light on their circumstances and what brought them to this imminent point. Drew went way way down the rabbit hole at some point and obviously couldn't find his way out. His note didn't help us. Lacking any rational explanations, reading these notes usually causes survivors to ask more questions rather than provide answers. And believe me when I say, to read a final note is painful beyond description. If you receive a final note, it is your right to read it or not, to believe it or not, to accept it or not.

Without a note discovered, we scour the premises and our memories for reasons to answer the WHY of it – we think that a note would have made everything clear as to their reasoning. We say, "Now we will never know", but in reality we would never know anyway. Succinctly stated in one of the many writings of the American Association of Suicidology (AAS), "How can a suicide note possibly explain the logic of a person who already believes suicide is a reasonable way to end the pain and suffering they have endured?" As a survivor, we are in a no-win situation - damned if you do have a final note, damned if you don't.

ENGAGE ALLOWING

Allow yourself the right to read the note or not, and allow that your emotions are going to be leading the way. If reading the note is what you must do, allow someone else that you trust implicitly to read it first for you. Allow them to be your safety net for the fallout that will come, and then allow your response to be what it is without explanation or censorship to anyone else including you. *Do what you must and do not apologize in any way for what you feel, what you decide and what it says.*

We allow that all things written or left unwritten by our loved one belongs to their irrational thoughts at the time of death. We allow that all statements made by our loved ones as to blame, causes, significance, and future predictions should not and cannot be embraced because, while it made perfect sense to them before death, it cannot find any rationale with us. We lay these explanations at the feet of a disabled mind and cannot hold them as truth. To that end, we allow our loved one to have their last say. It doesn't help us, but heaven knows after all they have gone through before they take their life, they have every right to say it, however they want to say it. What we do is to completely let go of blame towards anyone, especially ourselves and Let Love take its place.

Is this easy? Absolutely not. Is it necessary and can you do it? Absolutely it is and yes you can.

Religious issues

This may or may not be something you have had to grapple with since your loved one passed, but if you are practicing a religious faith or come from an ethnic background that has a significant influence on your spiritual journey, you may have encountered some stressful barriers to an already tragic event. Perhaps your faith does not accept suicide, and in fact condemns the act as a sin of the greatest magnitude. Your response may be that you are accepting of what your faith is telling you to practice, or you may discover that you are angry and resentful. Honor those responses and emotions at any given time when they occur. Allow yourself to experience it in the moment, but then deep breathe and let it release. If you so choose, you can make any decisions surrounding your spiritual guidance without needing to explain yourself. Your faith and religious guidance is up to you. Many practicing faiths today give greater understanding to the tragic outcomes of a less than well-functioning mind.

Drew was raised Catholic and we raised Drew and Emma to have a foundation in faith that hopefully would last them for their lifetime. The priest they grew up with helped us all with our joys and tragedies throughout our growing years, and he was there when Drew was sent Home. Our religious affiliations supported us fully and continuously during that time without administering judgment of any kind. That may not always be the case for you and you will have to decide what it is that you need from that corner of your life.

Engage Allowing

You allow that you may not get everything that you need from your religious affiliation and this is no one's fault. Perhaps it will make a difference to you and perhaps it will not affect your recovery whatsoever. *The choice to accept any foundational practices that reside on either side of the religious ball court, rests solidly on your side of the net. Anger will not serve your healing process, so if you are feeling adrift in what your faith can provide, allow others to be your unbiased support system in the moment and draw your strength from them.*

The Practice

1. Set aside a time of day and/or an amount of time within that day to consciously practice Allowing. You can make it as long or short as you wish, but try to schedule it when you will be interacting with others in some way. A variation could be watching a news program, but this scenario would probably not be as effective as personal interface.

2. Be aware of what is being said to you or around you. You needn't be an active part of the conversation, but it might be more compelling if you were.

3. Listen specifically for dialogue that may be controversial, opinionated, vastly different from what you think and feel, a topic that activates your emotions in some way such as anger, an opinion that you feel very strongly about, anything that inspires positioning or centers of polarization. An example statement from someone else might be: "Everyone who has red hair is either a hothead or an airhead." (Are you a redhead? Is your significant other a redhead? Are your children redheads?)

4. Try not to be judgmental about your emotional reaction, but recognize that you have one – identify

it. Do not act on defending how you are feeling about the interaction to yourself. Accept the fact you are experiencing a reaction that is triggering you. If you make your reaction seem wrong to yourself, you will feel a hit to your self-esteem if you allow others to project their values onto you. Their belief system is not your belief system.

5. Next notice how you may be setting up a protective posture to the other person, who does not think as you do. Are you being tempted to tell them they are wrong? Do you feel the need to verbally convince them or change their opinion? Does it feel as if it could become a "me-or-them" situation?

6. Receive by listening to the other person's opinion, choice, response, and reasons without forming a judgment. Become neutral. No one is telling you how you must view any topic.

7. Try to extract yourself at the conclusion of the discussion by acknowledging that they have an "interesting point of view."

8. This exercise can be exceptionally challenging when the topic under discussion is loaded with emotion on both sides.

9. Do your best and give yourself congratulations for making progress.

As a survivor, you will undoubtedly come up against this type of interaction on many an occasion. Remember, your ideas, opinions and beliefs are right for you. You never need to defend them to yourself or to someone else. If the others do not accept your thoughts as valid, that is their issue, not your issue. You are perfect just as you are.

CHAPTER 7

You Manifest What You Think

(The law of attraction)

"The mind is everything. What
you think you become."

— BUDDHA

"If you change the way you look at things,
the things you look at change."

— WAYNE DYER

MUCH HAS BEEN WRITTEN IN the last decades about the
law of attraction, but actually the principle has existed

for centuries, even millennia, traced back to ancient times, often in the teachings of Eastern philosophy. In the writings of Buddha, there is reference to this law: "All that we are is the result of what we have thought." In our modern society, there are many wonderful and brilliant authors supplying information about the law of attraction, and their writings are both inspirational and thought provoking. The law is the name given to the belief that "like attracts like" and that by focusing on positive or negative thoughts, one can bring about positive or negative results. If you accept that all things and thoughts have a vibration associated with them, then matching vibrations are pulled together. Within that theory is the understanding that people and their thoughts are both made from "pure energy," and that like energy attracts like energy. Deep and heady stuff, to be sure.

Simply stated, this principle is that you manifest what you think, every second of every day. It's never just been about wealth and material things, it is all things you bring into your life. Herein lies the possibility that as we think and engage in ideas that are important to us, we will draw or attract into our life and environment things that are the same as the very thoughts we put out to our mind and the Universe.

Words are important, and you know this from understanding Intention. If what you think and say is what you get—and I live every day as if there are no truer words—you need to initiate positive thoughts and then believe those thoughts, and finally use the words to make those thoughts become real. Fake it until you make it is not just a slogan; if you say it and think it until you believe it, you will manifest it.

Over my front door a few years ago there was this very small bird that chose to build a nest of mud up against the brick. Every day she would haul the mud up and try to connect it to the rough brick and as it dried it would fall off. Over and over again, day after day, I watched almost in agony as she tirelessly made her attempt only to have it land on my porch. It seems no one told her that this could not be done, because one rainy afternoon, somewhere between a miniscule piece of grout and a section of scrappy edge, it held. Within no time she had her mud nest and it balanced out into the air as if it was weightless. It seemed magical. I looked at it with such wonder and appreciation and felt I had learned a lesson from that tiny creature—the seemingly impossible can be done simply because you believe it will and expect it to.

Our thoughts and words have such power! If you watch children at play you can see how they have no barriers to believing what they are creating. There is no one to tell them that this is not possible, so they allow their brains to establish wonderful worlds and adventures that are fully real and they can experience. Once a child creates something, they believe it, expect it and let it in as their reality. The words they use to enact their play arena completely support what has been created in their minds. As adults we stand by in amazement at this ability, but never seem to use it ourselves. We left childhood imagination behind a long time ago.

As adults, we are taught to set barriers against our most wonderful, crazy creations, simply because, according to adult rules, they cannot exist and could never be. Often, this set of improbabilities is provided by our parents, other adults, society and the community. As we leave childhood behind we are already building and accepting screens to accomplishments, and setting them in place to tell us "rationally" why something is impossible or doesn't make sense in the "real" world.

HOW DOES THIS AFFECT US AS SURVIVORS?

This tool just may be one of the most important ones we will ever learn for daily life. It goes beyond being a survivor of suicide; it affects our lives as interactive beings on the planet. Come along with me here on the assumption, (even if it is a stretch for you), that what you are primarily thinking and saying in words is what you will manifest and receive. Our thoughts are powerful. The words that we use to support our thoughts are just as powerful. *So if we formulate the thought that we are guilty of not doing enough to save, discover and successfully deflect our loved one from taking their life, then the only thing we will manifest is guilt.* If on the other hand we choose a more positive possibility, with the strength of our little bird and her mud nest, which is to accept the fact that our interventions would not have changed the outcome. How might looking at our thoughts and the words we use to express those thoughts alter our ability to heal and greet tomorrow in a better frame of mind?

For those of us who are scientists at heart, there has been a fair amount of experimental work done on measuring the power of words and how they affect individuals and our environment. Dr. Masaru Emoto in his first publication, *The Hidden Messages in Water,* describes what happens to water crystals when they are exposed to damaging and toxic words, as well as those that are loving and nurturing. The photographs alone are astounding to see. If our language can have such an effect on water, I hesitate to imagine how great the impact of the spoken word to the human body, whether our body or someone else's. The human vessel is greater than 60 percent water.

Another author of significance is Pam Grout with her book *E2.* Ms. Grout's publication gives her readers the opportunity to participate in nine separate experiments, on their own, giving credence to the law of attraction. In each experiment, you are able to manifest that for which you are thinking or desiring, simply by following the steps. It is the personal attempt to prove that your thoughts and consciousness impact matter – your thoughts affect the physical world and you draw what you are focusing on to you.

If you embrace the belief that you will receive what you are thinking, and if you are contemplating what you don't want, you can be pretty sure that is exactly what you will get.

Putting that philosophy to work, let's consider another thought, one that manifests in the heads of survivors for years and years, sometimes for their entire life—that thought is, if we look hard enough and ask ourselves and others often enough, we will come to understand *why* they did it. We ask and ask and then worst of all, declare that we should have known. In the world of survivorship, this is the most negative of thoughts we will ever engage in. If we stay in this negative place, we can never heal simply because our thoughts say we should have known, and to that end we will forever believe we should have known. From this scenario, there will be no point from which we can escape the negativity of guilty thinking and guilt application. It will perpetuate itself indefinitely. This would be a good time to step through the looking glass and see our thinking and ourselves from the opposite side. You will remember in the chapter on Gratitude and Appreciation, that we *always* have the choice to change our perspective and view the scenario from a 180-degree position.

If we abide by the law of attraction, the energy we emote toward thinking that guilt by association is real, then we will bring, "like energy" of guilt into our lives. It will stay with us and get buried by us into the nether regions of our psyche and heart. Conversely, by having the thoughts that we are not responsible for the tragic outcome of our loved one's suicide, we automatically initiate a true healing cycle. Accepting guilt is negative, eliminating guilt is positive. Don't you want to accept what is positive for your life?

This is a good place for an example, one that we have used previously. Let's say you are trying to work with the insurance company that covered the life of the victim. Every time you pick up the phone to make yet another contact with them, the thoughts running through your mind as the extension is ringing are, "This will go nowhere yet again." You say to yourself, "I never get help or resolution from the insurance representative. We are going in circles and they continuously say 'no' to me about everything I ask for. No one is ever going to help me with this terrible situation!"

To illustrate, I will break down this internal conversation into all of the negative statements that are being engaged.

1. Going nowhere
2. Never getting help or resolution
3. Continuously say no
4. No one is ever going to help me
5. Terrible situation

What if, while that phone extension is ringing and you are waiting for the representative to answer, you say to yourself the following phrases:

* I *know* that this phone call will give me some information I didn't have before.
* The representative will listen to me and to what I need.
* I will hear "yes" today for something that I truly require.
* I will get some help today and they will assist me in this situation.

What do you think might happen here with this more positive thinking? Is it possible that you will make some headway that will be helpful and beneficial for you? And even if you still doubt the law, you will at least reduce your stress levels as you enter in the conversation with a positive attitude. *Like energy attracts like energy.* My positive thought vibration will bring positive response. What will you believe from here on, if you see you can actually manifest the assistance you so clearly asked for?

This is the point when you can begin to examine what you are thinking about on a moment-to-moment basis. What are *you* attracting right now? *Where* are your thoughts and *what* are your thoughts? Are you thinking about bringing stability to your world despite your current experiences or are you simply going through the motions because your world has been rocked to its core and everything you know for sure has changed? Are you expecting to find relief or do you think that happiness will forever elude you because of this tragedy?

Using the simple principle of the law of attraction, let's consider how we as survivors can use this strategy every day.

Assess the words you are using

As I talk with survivors, and in general with many clients who may not be survivors but are trying to comprehend and embrace the law of attraction, I notice that most often they begin their thought processes and general statements with words that describe *lack*. Here are some simple examples:

* ✿ I *wish I had...*
* ✿ I *don't see* how I can ever...

* I have already *missed* my opportunity to…
* I *don't have*…
* I *never have* all of the…
* I probably *never will* be able to…
* I *am not* in a position to…
* That is way too far *out of my reach*…
* That *can't* happen…
* I *can't* change now…
* I *can't* change that…
* I will *always be sad* or angry…
* Yeah, when pigs fly…!

You get the idea. Look at all of those italicized words and think to yourself how often your sentences start or contain them. If our thoughts are so powerful that what we say and think is what we get, then you will be satisfied with the best life has for you only when pigs fly.

INITIATE POSITIVE STATEMENTS

Just recently I saw a wonderful story reported on a television program that covered a young woman terribly injured in an accident that left her paralyzed from the chest down. She was engaged to a young man who spent his days giving her words of loving encouragement that in no way reflected her physician's expert opinion that she would never walk again.

He used words that spoke to her of only walking and feeling her legs again. And she did feel her legs in slow recovery. This courageous woman walked—with a cane—down the aisle on her wedding day. During torturous exercises during her recovery she was often asked if she was having a *bad* day – her answer would be, I am having a day. Powerful positive words support powerful positive thoughts.

Now let's rewrite those sentences to contain 180 degrees difference in their meaning, using positive language to state our point.

* I *have...*
* I *see* the way...
* I *expect* my opportunity to...
* I *always have...*
* I *have all* of the...
* I *will be* able to...
* I *am* in a position to...
* That is *within my reach...*
* That *will* happen, it *is happening* now...
* I *am* changing now...

* I *am* changing that…
* I am sad or angry sometimes, but then, *I always find my way…*
* Oh look! Pigs *can* fly!

BECOMING AWARE OF YOUR EMOTIONS

We have spent some time talking about how our emotional state is a measuring stick for what we are experiencing inwardly. As you cultivate awareness of your emotions, you will notice that how you feel will always affect your physical being, either positively or negatively. If we are fearful, our heart rate is elevated and our pulse may be racing, hands are sweaty and the sympathetic nervous system is entirely on alert. If we are angry, our blood pressure begins to climb quickly, logical thinking in our brain may begin to short-circuit, fists clench, stomach acid rises rapidly and our neck and shoulder muscles tighten. If we feel sad or guilty, stress can produce aching of the chest and heart area, less ability to hear or think clearly, stomach ache, and muscles and joints can become painful.

All of the above symptoms regarding fear, anger, and stress are being captured by our internal organs in a powerfully negative way unless we halt that process. Notice that I say "unless." That is, it *could* be very harmful to our body if we do nothing. Our emotions as internal barometers are good and purposeful. They tell us that something is causing us to react and the information we are learning is trustworthy. If we emotionally respond with fear, we recognize the need to evaluate and intercede on our own behalf by deep breathing, allowing and withholding judgment, perhaps locating the origin of the stressor and facing it. If our emotional response is joy, we recognize the positive effect on body, mind, and spirit and just go with it. It is what we do with this knowledge that will make the difference between healing and being stuck.

Returning to our earlier examples of negative statements such as "I don't have, I never have, I am not, I cannot," when you say these words, your emotions rise up as a co-conspirators, manifesting as hopelessness or sadness. You consciously understand this, you recognize it. That's the good part! If it doesn't feel good to say or hear these words and phrases, you can be quite sure your physical body will respond to them negatively as well. You will feel the sadness, shoulders will slump, posture depreciates via the spinal column, and then your brain comes back with, "See, I told you!"

Now is the perfect time for whatever...

This moment, right here, is known as perfect timing. This is when you recognize and are aware you are self-defeating your purpose to heal and you can do something about it. That is what it means to be aware. Prior to understanding of where you are right now, you were unaware, and took no countermeasures to move away from that kind of stuck-ness. Now you can. Look to your emotional reaction to your thoughts, and you will know immediately if you need to change your thinking. I refer you to the beginning of this section, to the quote by Wayne Dyer, "If you change the way you look at things, the things you look at change."

Now let's take the opportunity to look at typical scenarios and examples that we may encounter as survivors, and decide that we will respond with words that put our mind in a positive state and make a change that supports healing. Let's also assume that there will be others of the seven tools that can and should come into play to deal with the daily challenges, and use them in tandem with affirmative thinking and uplifting words. *All positive thinking when exercised consistently brings positive results.*

SCENARIO #1
The belief:

"I *can never go* to a survivor support group. I *will break down* in front of all those people and probably be *unable to talk* about anything that I feel; trust me, I will be completely tongue-tied. I *cannot listen* to all those tragic stories, *mine is bad* enough. Those groups *don't really help* you anyway; they only dredge up the *lost memories.*"

The analysis:

Looking at this situation from our mirror image, we can see that the survivor has set a barrier to seeing the advantages of group support. By looking at the words that the survivor uses to describe how they view the situation, it is clear that they see themselves in a position of lack. Additionally, the survivor has fear of being unable to contribute unless they keep themselves in emotional control at all times. Finally, there is the stigma that support groups are ineffective toward healing, perhaps because suicide has a stigma that doesn't encourage supportive dialogue.

Change the thinking:

No one should make anyone go anywhere – but if the decision is seen as a choice of yes/go or no/don't go, the survivor can be in control of how they work with their emotional responses and do so without labeling the outcome ahead of time. The survivor can *allow* for the fact that they may be uncomfortable or be emotionally exposed at this time and are just not ready. That's a good thing! And if they do decide to attend a support group, they can *allow* that emotional response is natural in being human, *be in the moment* and accept sadness that we all understand. They can be *grateful* that many survivors frequently find relief within such groups and wish them well, while knowing that this may not be in their own best interest right now. They can set an *intention* to be open to new information relating to group therapy and wait for answers to come.

SCENARIO #2

The belief:

"She was my best friend. You would think I *should have known* or seen something to give me a clue as to what was going wrong in her head. We talked all the time and told each other everything. I *can never* put that kind of trust into someone else ever again; it will hurt too much when you lose them. We loved to go to spinning class together every Saturday. Now I find no reason to go. The whole idea depresses me so badly; I *can't even find my way through it* and probably *never will*. I *hate* this! I *should have* been there for her!!"

The analysis:

The focus in this conversation surrounds presumed guilt and loss of trust. The survivor is somehow responsible and deceived at the same time. She feels she should have known all things and guided everyone through to safe waters, and now she feels she may never give trust another chance to be part of her social life. She is giving up a physical outlet that is labeled as tainted and has even introduced the word "hate" in her description of her experience.

Change the thinking:

Release guilt and *allow* that someone else's choices may be directly opposed and unacceptable to you, but fully contain their right to accomplish it their way. That alone directs you toward the path of *zero-judgment*. If we believe that trust is only permissible when we define it, then we set limits on when to trust. Instead, as survivors we can recognize that trust is and always will be an outcome that is obtainable again under new circumstances. Setting an intention that we are guilt-free is using a positive statement of being. If we love spinning or anything else, say so out loud and give permission to let it back into our lives when we are ready. The powerful words we use in our personal dialogue will *manifest what you think* as the outcome.

Scenario #3

The belief:

"I lost my husband to suicide eight years ago and I still do not understand what was *so wrong in our existence* that he took his life *away from me*. Every day I face the anger of being alone and *not even knowing* why I am alone. Always rising above the anger is the immeasurable sadness of *not having* him in my world anymore – we had so much ahead to do together. I know he also had physical illness as well as depression, but *where is the fairness* in that? *Everything I touch now seems to turn to crap*: my job, the *inability* to find social outlets, my weight, even my own health. All of it has been *going slowly downhill* since he died, and now my parent is ill as well. Just how much can I take before I break?"

The analysis:

The guilt and anger of the survivor is going strong and moving full steam ahead eight years after the suicide of her husband. Consider the long term effects on the body of continuous anger and shades of blame, both toward herself and her husband for leaving this world by choice. By focusing on "our existence," she declares that somehow she was a contributing factor in his decision. Many of the descriptions she uses to express her current state of mind and body center solely on lack. On the Richter scale this puts emotional and body system response perpetually high and in the danger zone. Physical deterioration and the inability for organic systems to cope are going to cause damage unless the survivor makes an intervention. The Survivor must break the pattern, not someone from the outside. Healing begins from within.

Change the thinking:

Using the *intention* tool that declares that the survivor is guilt-free is a conscious first step. She will have a tough time healing if she thinks she is responsible in any way. *Survivors are not responsible!* Anger is a smoldering fire that affects the psyche and physical body deeply. To work with anger, she may use *silence and meditation* long enough to put her anger on the table to look at it. She can acknowledge anger as a human emotional response and gently *release* the need to hold on to it. She can *allow* herself to be angry, and then let it go. She can try to think of all the things she had with her husband that were fine and good, focus on them and be *grateful* for the time they were together. Whenever the anger and guilt rise up, she can *deep breathe* through it and look at all the possibilities from the other side of the mirror. By observing from this vantage point, a survivor can be witness to opportunity for change.

What are you looking for as a survivor? Can you sincerely define what you desire, and *how would you say that out loud, using simple words that express clearly what you want to have happen?* Is it peace, or chaos? Is it love or engaging in hate? Anger or unconditional acceptance? Embracing or isolation? If words are ours to choose, then, as they were quoted in the 1989 movie *Indiana Jones and The Last Crusade,* "choose wisely." Because what you say is what you get; and if you really really want to have peace and love, unconditional acceptance and joy, then those are the words in your vocabulary. Leave the rest of them in some file that you no longer have to open.

THE PRACTICE

I will state outright that practicing positive thinking and using positive dialogue, even if it is just with you, is not easy to do or measure. How do we count how many times per day we say positive or negative things – to others and silently right within our own head? Measuring something like this is very much like herding cats; everything moves pretty fast in every direction. We talk and think faster than consciousness can follow. Our brains formulate sentences much quicker than our hands can record. That means it is a daunting task to first decide that the words you are using are negative, and second, to count them.

This practice works whether you are in conversation with another person—either through email, phone or face-to-face—or whether you are alone and in conversation with yourself, otherwise known as *your thoughts.* For the purposes of training, you could start with a witnessed conversation or written material. The reasons for beginning this way are so you can focus your attention on what negative words sound like in conversation outside of your own head. You will really have to tune up listening skills and do it for short periods of time.

1. Look at the clock and try to listen to someone's conversation for 3 to 5 minutes. Perhaps it is a very limited news program or interview; however you might want to stay away from television shows, since their dialogue can be extremely scripted and generally involves more than two people in the exposure. It might be a chat at a table near you in the coffee shop. We have all been in a position of proximity to overhear or even participate in any number of public situations, such as a train ride, restaurant, elevator, or subway. If your circumstance feels something akin to eavesdropping, you certainly can make your own decision as to moving somewhere else. On the whole, most public conversations are benign and not expected to require privacy by the participants, or else they would sit somewhere else. Be gentle with self-criticism on how well you can do this the first few times. Dialogue is often tough to follow, and if the individual words are passing you by, then try to collect the tone or

vibrational feeling from the encounter you are "observing." Does it raise an emotion in you? Is it positive or negative?

2. Part 1: Make a real or mental tick mark each time you hear a word or phrase that could be categorized as *negative* or perhaps describing a *lack of.* If necessary look again at the examples on page 106 under the heading "Assess the words you are using" There you will see common ones we utter every minute of every hour, without thinking. At the end of the assigned minutes, if you have been as diligent as possible, you can get some inkling of how much and how often the participants were entertaining "lack of" in their thoughts and speech. Were you able to understand how the subjects were representing their desires via their speech and could you imagine what they would expect to receive in the future because of it? This is the law of attraction or *You Manifest What You Think.* (For a brilliant example of this watch the film, *The King's Speech* with Colin Firth. The more that King George feared, the more his speech faltered. It was when his coach was able to teach him positive associations with speaking in public, that he was able to turn his perceived lack into abundance. When words were the enemy, the King suffered, but when the words became his friend, he shined.)

3. (Note: It is not only what one person's words can bring to themselves, but also how their words, when directed toward another, can affect that person's experience.)

4. Part II: If you felt you were able to follow the encounter well enough, perhaps you could select another brief encounter, but this time make a tick mark for every positive thought, word or phrase in the same way as Part I. Which category gets the biggest number of marks? What could the subjects be magnetizing to their experience now, based on a positive dialogue?

5. Part III: Once you are familiar with the words and thought phrases that you need to be, be very aware of short conversations that you have with yourself or someone else and do it on a limited basis. What words are in your vocabulary? What do you pick up and can mentally tick off from your verbal partner or yourself? We are all familiar with people who seem to have fully biased and/or negative dialogues with everyone. When you are comfortable with thinking and talking in the positive most of the time, this is a turning point for you, because you find you need to remove yourself from those who can't. Eureka!

6. This awareness is built very gradually. Be patient with your ability to learn hearing in your

own dialogue, and those of others, as to how it is matching up to the law. Practice every day, and develop your listening skills steadily. Before you realize it you will intuitively be recognizing a conversation that reflects the desirable rather than the undesired. It's all in the words and thoughts we send out.

We become accustomed to speech, (our own and the speech of others) that supports what we *think* we are lacking. We hear it repeatedly and regurgitate it back out as thoughtless truth. We have the chance to break that pattern by being aware of our words and how we use them for ourselves and toward others.

CHAPTER 8

The Now Moment: Be In It And Experience It

> "You must live in the present,
> launch yourself on every wave, find your
> eternity in each moment."
>
> — HENRY DAVID THOREAU

BACK IN THE SECTION ON silence and meditation, I introduced a type of meditation called mindfulness, where you were being very present in what you were thinking and feeling, using absolutely no energy whatsoever toward judgment. Additionally, mindfulness should not entertain any thoughts surrounding what has taken place in the past or what might happen in the future. In this state, we are not worrying about how we will feel in thirty minutes from now or what we felt emotionally ten days ago. Mindfulness is one great meditational way to be in the now moment.

Being in the now moment simply means being acutely mindful of what is happening in our experience at this very second. It is now, whether we are afraid, peaceful and still, angry, joyful, or in bliss. We recognize the emotion or feelings we have, and we are looking at them as they are occurring in our life at this very minute, but observing them, accepting their existence without responding. Most importantly, the now moment is not judged as being good or bad, right or wrong, acceptable or unacceptable. It just is. Being in the now does not involve doing something or anything; it is just "Being." I am sure you have heard that term before. If you are in a state of mindfulness, you are giving all of your active attention to the present and therefore, living in that very moment.

I found a wonderful article by Erin Lanahan, about being fully present in the moment, entitled "Freedom Is Where My Feet Are." (Please see the reference section.) The enduring message she describes is that if we feel chaotic or overwhelmed, we can simply focus on our feet. By doing this simple task, we can start again to be in the present. I love this! As my mind churns away with what I have done or left undone, or what I have waiting for me looming on the horizon, by seeing my feet, I can return to home base. My feet are on the grass, they are in my favorite shoes, they are touching warm sand, my toenails are painted bright happy red, my feet are tanned from the sun. You get it – *I am right here, right now and paying attention to my feet.* It stops me from awful-izing, it keeps me on solid ground and rests my crazy hungry thoughts, it allows me to breathe properly simply from awareness. It is very, very alive!

A Drew Story

The second appearance from Drew came approximately two and one-half months after he passed. My dear friend and I had decided to spend a long weekend at an acquaintance's home in the mountains. There is a small lake there, surrounded by large cliffs; it's a favorite of both locals and out-of-towners alike because the clear spring-fed lake looks like glass. After a Friday night sleep, we decided to select one of four possible spots to spend Saturday, but it had to be near freshwater – this lake being one of the options on our list. Three of the choices were to the left of the T in the road, while the lake –which was a bit further—was to the right. My dear friend suggested we check out the closest ones first but I was convinced that the lake should be our destination.

My friend was fine with that choice, so made our way to this lovely lake setting without even considering the other three spots. For some unexplainable reason, the lake was where I needed to go – I literally heard, "Go right".

We were first to arrive, the only other person there was a National Forest Ranger and perhaps Smokey the Bear himself. We had every single choice available as to where to set up our picnic and we selected a great table by the water and within sight of the cliffs on the other side of the lake. On the beach were huge logs that one could sit on and read or just enjoy the view and this is exactly where I placed myself with my e-reader. The odd thing is that I couldn't seem to get started reading and instead gazed over the clear glass water to the granite cliffs on the other side. I could see some of the impressions in the granite and a small crag-like area on the left of the cliff, a third of the way from the top. What looked like a green bush was growing from some area in the middle. Additionally, there was a tiny ledge that appeared to be, from my distance, about a hand in width.

More families began to arrive and over the next half hour the beach area filled with day-trippers and blankets and picnics. There was an area on the beach to my left that curved around that I couldn't see. As I lazily watched all of this gentle activity, felt the sand underneath the soles of my feet and stared onto the surface of the water following the diamonds reflected by the sun, Drew appeared in front of me levitating above the water with his left side facing me. From the waist down he was cloudy and indistinct, but from his waist upwards all about his outline was crystal clear. His chest and left shoulder were lean and just as I remember. All the features of his face were perfect, as were his hands that I have always admired and memorized so well. I would have recognized him by his beautiful hands alone.

Drew said, "Beautiful isn't it?"

I was dumbfounded. He was talking to my mind.

"Yes, it really is" I said.

He asked, "Would you like to go up?"

Without a second's hesitation, I answered that I did.

The next moment I found myself hovering on the right side of the cliff –in the air—and I reached out and touched the wall of the granite side. "Wow I am levitating!" I could feel each little stone that made up the wall, and it was so cool to the touch. I also noticed that the ledge I had seen from below was actually wide enough to stand on, not the span of a human palm. The bush I had seen was in truth a very small tree growing right out of the side of the rock from a small crevice. The crag-like area on the left was a small cave that had previously been used to harvest some of the granite in many years past. As I turned my head, I looked down at my place below on the log. There I was with my book in my lap!

I glanced down to the part of the beach that was not visible to me as I sat below and realized it had a lot of families and children filling up the space. There was a blue cooler and a red bathing suit all within sight from above. There was a path that came out to the pebbled area of the lake and I didn't know it was there before.

I could feel that Drew was somewhere close to me but saying nothing.

"I love this!" I said to him. "I cannot believe what I am seeing!"

I was up in the air, but sitting down below at the same time. I excitedly wondered if we could just do this anytime we wanted to. Before I knew it, I was back in my sitting spot and Drew was again hovering over the water with his left shoulder toward me.

I asked, "What are you doing here?"

His answer was, "I am watching over him," and he pointed to the cliff.

At the base of the cliff was a full stand of pine trees running along the ground and obliterating about a quarter of the lower cliff itself. I looked and saw nothing, no-one. Drew inferred that he was on an "assignment." It was something I simply understood. Then he was gone. On assignment, I said to myself – could it be that those who have crossed over to new energy can be on duty, working? What a concept, I thought without censure. Did I think that spirits simply roamed and roamed and played a harp all day or could it be that they have opportunities to guide, guard and stand watch? When Drew had been laid off from his professional position some years back, I can recall that he sat in front of his computer for 9 to14 hours a day researching jobs and submitting résumés. What an effort, it was exhausting. So here he was now hovering over the water and saying casually that he's on assignment? Where was the big job search? Where was the angst over getting work again? Where was the need for a headhunter? And yet here he was probably doing the biggest job needed in the Universe!

In my case, could a monumental intervention of the great unknown have just occurred? Is it possible I was allowed to peek into one of the greatest mysteries contemplated by man? Are the Drew's of that plane ready to give us a guiding touch when we are in a tough or precarious spot? Every once in a while can't we "feel" someone close to us, protectively?

For thirty minutes I just stared at the cliff thinking that I was missing something— someone I couldn't see due to distance. As I watched, over the crest of the tree line came two rock climbers, slowly working their way up the side of the granite. I jumped up and yelled, "There he is!" I actually borrowed a pair of binoculars from a neighboring family and found there were two climbers going up together. Apparently Drew was responsible for one of them. Some short time later, my friend and I took the path walk all around the parameter of the lake. To my surprise, the hidden beach area—the place we couldn't see from our picnic spot, but one I could see from my "elevation" to the stone face—had a family there with a blue cooler and a little girl in a red bathing suit.

If I had let my thoughts be anywhere but in the now moment, I don't believe I ever would have been able to experience this encounter. I know that as sure as I know the sun will rise in the morning. Drew came to me, I believe, because I was already in the moment and seeing exactly where my feet were. I was in the now moment and he could connect with me being there.

LEARNING TO HEAL IN THE NOW MOMENT

How can this now moment tool work positively for us as survivors? We use *now* as a way to view and measure our progress in healing. What do I do with a now moment when I go out there in the world? How can it help me in my dealing with tragedy, in my dealing with daily stressors? Said more simply, how can being in the moment assure us that we are healing? I would like to use some guided imagery to prove a point in trying to answer that question. My goal is to illustrate that with dedicated belief in being thoroughly present in the moment, we can feel secure that change for the better is taking place because we feel it. We feel it and experience it accurately as now.

As you read the following paragraphs, picture yourself in the scenario, participating in the activity. Water is a good example of healing; it is a cleanser of wounds, it represents rebirth and it washes us free from unwanted debris. Let's take a silent and meditative trip to the ocean. Walk on the beach and feel how the warm sand is shifting gently under each foot step. Is it packed hard because of its proximity to the water's edge or very soft and pliable further back? Now look out over the vast body of water that faces you, do you know whether the tide is coming in or going out? Unless you are a mariner, or routinely follow the tidal information before stepping out of your house, by just standing at the water's edge and putting your feet in the surf, it is pretty tough to know what the tide is doing at that moment. I have made the decision for you here, the tide is coming in. From this point, you have six hours to just stand there and be in the presence of one of Earth's greatest natural achievements.

* As the water rises to touch your feet, you take the opportunity to consider how refreshing and soothing it embraces your skin. You set the intention that you will engage every physical

connection you possibly can to soothe your body with these simple yet loving sensations provided by nature. Formulated well, your Intention will automatically address the stressors that are encountered each day as a survivor, such as worry, guilt and painful anticipation. You feel the surf pulling at your toes and soles, little sucking movements that begin to undermine the weight of your body. Because of the law of attraction, your Intention removes the negative thoughts from you and takes them out to sea. You are standing in a powerful positive environment.

* The clear water surrounds your ankles, one of the very joints that ache with discomfort from time to time, and you realize that you can already move them more easily in this ocean water than you ever could on pavement without it. Your ankles are weightless. You feel how grateful you are that you have discovered a reprieve, and you imagine that it will last as long as you want it to, just by your positive thought commitment. You hold on to these visions since they seem to reflect everything you want in your life.

* The tidal waters continue to come in ever so slowly and steadily, engulfing your calves and thighs and you contemplate the abundance of muscles you have at your disposal for walking

and running, climbing and moving. These very muscles are helping you keep your balance as the water deepens around you. Your feet and legs shift as the ocean water pushes you this way and that. What a gift you have been given in that all muscular adjusting you make to procure your balance, since it happens without ever having to think about it. Perhaps you never quite considered it before. So you say "Thank you," to no-one in particular in appreciation for the magnificence that your body represents.

❋ As the ocean level reaches your abdomen and chest, you conceive the displacement of liquid, however small, that you can accomplish simply by deep breathing and stretching your face skyward. It is so easy and so fulfilling as you take in the beautiful clouds that are rolling above you. Your exhalation blends with the air that is caressing your face and arms and becomes one with the Universe. Is your out-breath the same color as the air above you or have you changed its color to make it visible? You fill your lungs and roll backward, extending your arms out to either side of you and let your legs rise up to meet the water's surface. You release. You rest in the here and now and let everything go. You are completely supported.

✳ Here is the point where you place your complete trust in yourself and the law of attraction and nature. You are floating, and you are doing it without effort because you are being supported by something else – the dedicated belief in self-love, positive thought and the knowledge that change is taking place – that healing is taking place. In this one small act, you know without a doubt you are secure in the moment of time we call now. By putting your mind into what has happened and gone wrong in the past, or what unknown agendas lurk in the future, you might sink like a stone. But you won't, because you are using all of the tools to be in the now moment. That is the healing. You know how to avoid the harmful negativity that can invade your thinking, and change the way you experience life and your role within it.

Welcome back. Doing *now* feels really good, doesn't it?

THE "INITIAL" GRIEF IS A NOW MOMENT OF THE ROUGHEST KIND

Up to this point we have been discussing now moments that you can engage in whenever you wish, as often as you wish. We can even use them as meditation opportunities that use focus a little differently than still mind or silence does, by actually feeling intimately that which touches us. Another form of now which can occur, is one in which we are being in the moment, but it may not be a moment we want to *be* in, given a choice.

When we learn that we have lost someone to suicide—or any other traumatic loss—there is no escaping that event or the time surrounding it and following it. Our survival starts immediately. That time is unthinkable, unmanageable and painful beyond description. We could argue that when it took place it was indeed a now moment, but it represented chaos and loss of control of everything around you. It looks nothing like the now moments discussed above. This particular *now* cannot possibly represent engagement in healing on any level that is explainable. What we should recognize is that in the moment of despair, we face responses that are real and vital to experience, even as they happen. We can attempt to run or hide from the event; however, ten minutes or ten years from ground zero it will still be there. What we could do, if we were able, is to be acutely aware of what we felt during the aftermath. Truthfully, that is almost asking too much of ourselves, since it is at this point that our consciousness is making a herculean effort to protect us. The most common reactions are denial, memory loss or blurring of information, even confusion and disorientation. Our survivor mode kicked in spontaneously – fight or flight.

Yet, within some unpredictable period of time, which is likely different for everyone, we began to understand intuitively that the aftermath moments have receded, and new moments are beginning to take their place. Perhaps you became aware that you are on your own. Everyone has gone home and returned to their lives somehow, and you are left behind. The confusion and disorientation were gone, but perhaps anger and guilt have filled the screen.

Experiencing and recognizing these changes and the subsequent feelings, fears and emotions is important. Somewhere back then where your survivorship began, you likely denied yourself the now space, and it was just because you needed a safety net in the crisis. That net was your fight or flight mechanism doing what it does. Perhaps now it is time to use the now moment to let crucial emotions come in again.

That requires putting your feet where you can see them. (Remember the analogy, you can just look down and see your feet – what your feet look and feel like.) You can choose to allow the emotions to rise surrounding the loss, and greet them uncensored. Allow for it, surrender to it, especially if you never allowed yourself to do it before. Welcoming it even unwillingly, means you are not burying it, because once buried it is not easily resurrected, and it could become grief that continues endlessly.

And if that part of your first weeks and months become buried, and you are determined not to touch them ever again either consciously or unconsciously, I would like to suggest that there may be other ways, with the help and presence of licensed people who could assist you with that. As a nurse and survivor, I have only my experience, challenges and successes to use as guidance. You need to decide.

MY PERSONAL STORY

Welcome to my nightmare. Day Number One will forever be where the shit storm began. The moment after minimal comprehension occurred, was the beginning of the emotional roller coaster, and where my personal grief-to-healing, or immediate lack of it, first kicked in. There was no sugarcoating the fact that the start of that Day is not now, nor will it ever be like any other day in my life.

It began with the knowledge that my son did not come home the night before, he did not go to work that morning, and no one had heard from him or had any idea where he was.

My first emotion—disbelief—insanity simulated. I screamed at the heavens. Let him just drive into the yard, let him be unconscious but able to be saved, let him be anything but beyond reach. I promise anything and everything I own. I will give my life in exchange— so gladly, right now.

He was located, but not retrievable.

My second emotion—unlimited fear—unabated panic. My daughter was lost and running, and I had to stop her because she was what I had left and she wanted immediate answers that no one was going to give us.

Disbelief – this is stuff in books and on screen, not in my real life!

Confusion – what was the investigator saying to me, asking of me?

Disorientation – I am staring and staring at a table that has no meaning to me whatsoever.

My now moment, like yours, doesn't seem to compute very well. What I do recall is that even in the midst of chaos, I heard a voice that said, "Do this the very best you can right now, make your feet move in some direction right now, stop Emma from going up those stairs now. The baby is still in the stroller and someone must keep watch over her now. The rest will just have to take care of itself."

I was, like you, in a now moment I never asked for. Survival had kicked in, but it was a fight or flight mechanism. Later, I would not begin to comprehend exactly when the change from initial reaction to secondary reactions would happen, but it was well after all of the family, friends and kind attendees had gone home. Several weeks or months, it is a bit hard to recall, but I did know I was on my own. The choice to begin the healing process was not going to be initiated or managed by someone else, and the only person in my line of sight was me.

Perhaps you are thinking at this point that your personal circumstances of discovery have set you apart from the rest of the group of survivors, and indeed we all have our story, but this is somehow the moment that each survivor shares with all other survivors. It is part of our memory bank and cannot be extracted or erased. What I will say is that however you first gained the knowledge that your loved one took action against themselves, we all had to go through that moment of realization, that fight or flight. While the path of discovery may vary, the outcome is the same, and it is at this juncture that we must begin our journey toward healing. I wish I could change it for all of us, but I can't and no one else can either, so forward we must move.

When the initial activities subsequent to loss are ended, and everyone has left the building and returned to their own lives, you are left with disbelief and inability to even move. Nothing in your lifetime will ever ever, ever be this painful. This time period presents a pivotal point, where you can make a hole or make a path.

There are many professional people who can help you on your pathway to healing, and often this is the time to let them take some of your burdens under their wing. Ultimately, much of your journey will be in your own hands. The emotions that emerge in you may *feel* out of control, but they actually become your *new safety net.* This is where the now moment can be your friend, because truly being in the now moment requires that you experience everything fully. It is your glorious opportunity to unwillingly welcome what seems the most difficult. It is your right of passage. Choosing to make a hole will only bury your emotional outlets deeper and deeper, and it comes with consequences. And don't let anyone else move you through this emotional hurricane at a speed that suits them either with comments such as, "You must bear up for the kids. You must have known this could happen. Didn't you have some indication, any indication? What are we going to do now? How are we going to handle this; we can't tell the people that we know; don't say anything about suicide."

In order to witness life, one must live in the moment. The response to loss like this is heartbreaking, but to shuffle it backward to what conceivably went wrong or forward to what unknowns are yet to come is leaving the now moment suspended. *The now moment, done properly at this painful juncture, involves witnessing our thoughts, engaging them, feeling them fully as if they were pure sound.* To place a judgment on your thoughts at this time would be labeling them as good or bad when they are neither. Your thoughts are your thoughts; they are connected to reactions and emotions during the course of experience, and your emotions are what they are. Remember the fight or flight syndrome? After the biologic fight or flight is over, your body is doing what your body under extreme stress will unfortunately do - it is still responding. Don't leave the acknowledgment of response (wanted or unwanted) behind by leaving the moment behind. I am living proof that in the course of suicide loss and recovery, acknowledging your own reactions to any internal or external stimuli and coming to resolution, is like standing in the sun after a long winter. This is Hope in its purest form.

A CLIENT'S NOW MOMENT OPPORTUNITY

Let me share with you an example of a now moment smack in the middle of fear and worry. I have a friend whose wife has suffered one cancerous setback after another. Every treatment has such hope attached to it, even from the physician's point of view, and then something fails to have the desired outcome and they return almost to square one. My friend could not find words to express his fear of losing his wife, and so he was slowly slipping into a deep pocket of anxiety and depression.

It was nearly immobilizing him from day to day. He told me that he was unable to contemplate his future without his wife being in it. I could see he would not acknowledge the emotions he had surrounding death, and ultimately it all got in the way of his enjoying life on any given day.

He came to me for some help with his thinking. He realized that he was pulling his wife's healing and optimism down because of the depression he was experiencing in their situation, and he simply didn't know how to move away from it and truly help her. Medically, he was being treated for his anxieties, but he wanted to know what he could do to feel more positive around his wife.

Each time I work with someone and the seven tools it usually becomes clear to me early on which tools should come first. Intention and deep breathing are always high on the list because they work in tandem with all the other five tools, but generally there is one tool that will stand out for each individual that could decidedly make a difference. For this man I could see that he struggled to engage with his wife moment to moment because of all of his fears.

I asked my client what sort of things he liked to do and what his hobbies and interests were. While his wife was the primary gardener in the family, his choice was to take photographs that were worthy and unusual. It got me to thinking that being in the now moment was something that my friend could use as an important tool to keep some of his fears –of losing her and being alone— in perspective. I suggested that he spend time with his wife while she worked in the garden. Perhaps he could take close-up photos of her hands while she focused on a certain flower or plant, even while she was digging in the soil. Create a special exposure that really captured her diligence and talent, then develop and frame the pictures especially. Share them with her, showing her how he values her wonderful gifts. He could make it a joyful experience for both of them, while giving them time together.

This is being in the now moment: the moment he spends with his wife; the moment he captures that photo of her fingers on the petals of a lovely plant, nurturing and encouraging its growth, showing her love and value; the moment they are close together, both doing something they really love and at the same time! It is a positive step and creating positive and beautiful thoughts for the future. Right now, not maybe later when changes might be ahead … Here is the appreciation that will be sustained through photography for always, whatever that future brings. Appreciation, gratitude and abundance all demonstrate how they can work together to bring joy, even while they live under an umbrella of doubt.

OPENING UP THE MEMORIES

When you have someone in your life, you have memories. Whatever they are, they are yours for always to keep and cherish, remember and love. As in all things human, our memories of one another become so much more precious when our loved one has passed. Somehow the memories that surround a suicide victim seem harder to find purchase in our hearts than other losses. It hurts to let them in and it is nearly impossible to do it with joy. It runs on the rim of the unspeakable, so we must work harder at making them a regular part of our lives, if we do at all, because it makes all the questions arise, yet again. We must find a way over that.

We are the voice and living spirit of those who have passed from us, so we need to rethink how we can make all of the memories continue to be a part of our life without feeling like we are getting crushed under the weight of remembering what we no longer have in front of us. If we as survivors are terribly uncomfortable revisiting wonderful events, photos, films, artifacts and memorabilia of our loved one, we cannot expect anyone else to be comfortable with it either. Let's change that by making a new place for everything, starting with the Heart Hole.

As time progresses, that enormous empty space in our heart from suicide loss has found some way to soften at the edges, but if we are honest with ourselves, we know that the hole is fully still there. What if we took each memory, each item and artifact that belonged to them and us, forever connected, and place it safely and securely into that opening? Call this ceremony if you want, but it can work for you. We can use love and *Allowing*, *Gratitude* and *Release* to do it. Here is how it can be done.

I have a photo of Drew, playing a guitar, in a very particular plaid shirt that he loved, looking like a Bruce Springsteen in front of his own fireplace. What a scrunched up bearded Rocker's face he is making! Not his most beautiful pose for sure, but demonstrating his craziness for the dramatic. After Drew died, the material of that shirt was made into a hugging bear and the photo was placed in a plain silver frame. They reside on my dresser, and when I am cleaning my bedroom, I put on rocker music, hug the bear and dance, all while dusting the furniture. What a four-for-one deal in my heart hole! The bear, the hug, the music and the fabric. I have made it ceremony and I share it with anyone who sees it because it is and was a great memory worth keeping, and not just to myself. Share, share, share the memory. Every time you don't run from a memory and instead declare its value to others, you are filling precious space in the heart with good things.

Find a memory and allow (yourself) that there may be some pain and sadness attached to it for the most obvious of reasons. Share that memory with others, and allow that others may have some discomfort with it initially. However, the more value you place on the memory the more value others will attribute to it as well. Express gratitude for having the memory at all costs— it is a gift. What if you didn't have it in the first place? How truly sad that would be, so give it the incredible appreciation it deserves and cast that net far and wide. Finally, find the strength and will to release the sadness that you have attached to it—for it is certainly your emotion that is keeping it from filling that hole in your heart. The emotion is not being denied, it just comes, but after recognizing it and accepting it, then let it go. Mentally and ceremonially place it forever in that wonderful softened space and watch your resilience grow as you continue on the healing path. What an accomplishment of power and positive affirmation! Job well done.

JUST ONE OF DREW'S NOW MOMENTS—HE HAD SO MANY!

Perhaps fifteen or sixteen years ago, I took my family, sans Emma who was in school, to my hometown for a visit. For fun we went to a beautiful and incredibly large zoo for the day, and with everyone together, it couldn't have been more exciting. One of the grandest of the exhibits was a penguin house that contained every single type and kind of species, all of them different and unique in their look and characteristics. There were about seven of us all standing together in front of the great glass enclosure. The lodging for the penguins was extravagant and very well planned out. There was water, slides, ice structures, small caves and lots of light and air.

The Emperor penguin with such beautiful fancy cresting on his head stood at the top of one of the ice pieces—so grand and commanding. Various other penguins in different sizes and colors skittered about, looking as if they were really doing something important.

At this moment, Drew had decided to create a penguin sitcom by watching and anticipating movements they might make. Suddenly, from the middle of our family group I heard Drew's voice take on a somewhat authoritative voice. While he was positioned right up front at the glass enclosure, he stood very still and began to speak while looking at all the penguins in front of us and said, "Perhaps you are wondering why I called this gathering today. Cecil, please take your seat, and all of you pay attention, we are about to begin the board meeting." Drew could do a stand-up comedy routine without notice. While confronting his emotions was not something that he could do easily, doing what we were about to witness was almost second nature and truly one of his gifts.

A small penguin came running up near the Emperor penguin, whom we will call The Boss. Boss said to small penguin, "Wait a minute Allen, where do you think you are going? We need lunch orders taken right now. I will have a salmon on rye." Amazingly, "Allen" stopped in his tracks and just looked at the boss. Allen then touched close to several other penguin members of the meeting and from his movements appeared to be gathering the menu list. Not one of us could believe what we were seeing since everything that came out of Drew's mouth fit perfectly with the action behind the glass. We proceeded to dissolve into fits of laughter! Another bird came into the scene and Drew said in a very whiney voice, "Hey, George is sitting in my seat!" To which Drew, throwing out yet another voice for George, replied, "Didn't you get the memo? You aren't even in this meeting; you are in the one down the hall. You never read your memos, George." Unbelievably, at that moment George turned around and waddled in the other direction. To say we all were laughing so hard, tears were rolling down our face is an understatement. I was in great danger of requiring a change in underwear by this time, and other visitors to the zoo were starting to join the group because they wanted to know what was going on that was so funny on our side of the penguin house.

Allen had now reappeared and moved around other penguins and Drew piped up, "Ok, here is the herring salad. Boss—your salmon on rye, the kelp on pumpernickel - no mustard..." The group around us had swelled to maybe 18 to 20 people and they were in hysterics. I cannot remember any specifics about the rest of the zoo visit, but that penguin house story is as clear in my memory as if it happened three minutes ago. I belly laugh now at the thought. An entire "company board meeting" came to life on the other side of the glass and lasted for at least ten minutes without a single pause. Drew never missed a dialogue or opportunity. To this day, I have no idea how he did it – it was pure genius and luck.

If ever Drew was in the now moment, he was then. I cherish it as one of my sweetest and funniest memories ever.

Doesn't this story and all of the stories still make me laugh? Can't I laugh just as hard and loud as I did before – they are still funny! Can't I share all of these episodes with others so they know who Drew was? Why should I ever let my personal grip on grief and sadness allow me to give them up? These memories epitomize who Drew was and what his blessings were to us. I must not ever give them up, nor should you sacrifice your memories either because of grief

PRACTICE: FEEL THE STONE, CLICK THE SHUTTER

Here are some opportunities for being in the now moment that you can try as practice. Don't be deceived at how simple they may seem. Learning to arrest your brain from thinking backward or forward and only "seeing" what is immediately in front of you requires some behavior changes.

1. Doing your exercise routine: change to walking outside and do not wear an iPod or ear buds or cell phone. As you walk, feel what the surface of the path or road feels like and describe it in your mind. Deep breathe in some air deeply through your nose. What does it smell like? Is someone burning wood or can you pick up on floral, moss or other greenery? Feel the movement of your hips and breath, and get a sense of the rhythm that is created. Look to the left and right of you, what colors are most prominent as you move forward? Look ahead of you and decide if what you see is worthy of a photo; if you see something that you like, click the shutter in your head and put it in your memory. Pick up a chestnut or stone and hold it in your hand. Where are the ridges on it, the smooth sides, what size is it, what hand does it fit best in?

2. Go to the beach and remove your shoes. Push your feet deep into the sand and feel it squish up between your toes. Is it wet? Is it cool or very warm? Where is the sun in relation to where you are sitting or standing and how is it making

contact with your skin? What about the sound of the waves, big, small, loud, quiet? Walk on the part of sand that almost touches the water. Feel the step-push, step-push as you make your way along. Count how many steps it takes to get from one stone marker to the next? Pick up a stone, click the shutter.

3. If you are riding on a train or bus or other transportation, look at people around you. Take this time to put down your phone or tablet and simply be in the same space as those you see. What do you notice? Are they all swaying in the same direction as the car moves? How many are smiling? Describe to yourself the people waiting on the platforms of the stops along the way. Is that last train station a perfect image of the ones in a magazine for some reason? Click the shutter.

4. Start or enter a conversation with someone. Notice their eyes; what color and shape are they? How expressive is this person when they talk to you? Are you close together or far apart? Where are you most relaxed when standing in their presence? What is the topic you are discussing; is it something you know about or are you learning new information? Perhaps you would like to think about it more later; click the shutter. How are you listening, are you listening? Are they

listening to you? Where is your focus? Does this interaction feel comfortable like a stone in your palm? Where are the smooth or rough surfaces?

Mark Nepo, a writer and poet created a beautiful publication called *The Book of Awakening*. In the foreword to his book, Mark has been described as having a "passionate enthusiasm for sucking the marrow out of moments..." I will quote here a very poignant line about the now moment as he envisioned it: "Grateful and awake, ask what you need to know now, Say what you feel now. Love what you love now."

CHAPTER 9

The Long Haul

"May God break my heart so completely
that the whole world falls in."

—MOTHER TERESA

"Sorrow prepares you for joy. It violently sweeps
everything out of your house, so that new joy can
find space to enter. It shakes the yellow leaves
from the bough of your heart, so that fresh, green
leaves can grow in their place. It pulls up the
rotten roots, so that new roots hidden beneath
have room to grow. Whatever sorrow shakes from
your heart, far better things will take their place."

—RUMI

EVERYONE AT SOME POINT IN life sustains loss. And while survivors of suicide loss are painfully unique, all loss leaves its mark on us. Healing from any loss will take its own time manifesting back into our lives. It depends on a great many factors, and I believe we can be quite sure that the journey is never what we think it will be, even if we do have all the tools necessary to guide us. Recovery from suicide of a loved one has gigantic speed bumps, some of which you never see coming. The potholes could swallow you right up unless you truly remember that you carry around a fantastic GPS just waiting to provide your navigation around and through it all. This loving system gives you the confidence to settle in for the long haul, only if you use it consistently, wisely, and without restraint. Keep the system plugged in at all times if you possibly can, so it can alert you to the areas that you need to circumnavigate safely.

What exactly is The Long Haul? It is simply that as we move through our lives after loss, moment by moment, day to day, year after year, we should choose the healthiest and most positive ways to interact with ourselves and others, regardless of all the influences that come from the external world. This journey of healing can only begin from within Us; and if we believe in what we do and think for ourselves, the changes we experience for the better will be very obvious to others we encounter. It will radiate from us like an aura. It will emanate from us as vapor does when a cold rain hits a hot surface. It also means that if you have embraced the nature of the tools revealed in this book and operate from the center of your heart, you will always be heading in the direction of love and peace, for yourself and everyone around you. We can not only change how we view and handle the challenges, but we can strongly influence how people around us handle them as well. We are capable of being a positive force in creating a new foundation in the discussion of suicide – we can make a dent in the stigma that continually surrounds the public's suspicions and lack of compassion. By being our own role model for survivor healing, we become role models for the community at large. To do it effectively, we must use the tools effectively.

Generally, these tools are used in tandem with each other, two or three at a time, because each encounter often contains components that require more than one tool to work it through. You can use each one alone, but they are extremely effective working together. I began to discreetly introduce that strategy toward the end of Tool #6 *you manifest what you think*, and continuing in Tool #7, *The now moment*. In *the now moment*, I attempted to illustrate how the tools can interact with you as you interact with the world. The tools can cooperate as your team. The Long Haul is where you can make that occur purposefully.

During my time with so many other survivors, I heard their stories, we shed tears together and they all deposited pearls of wisdom to me that I will never forget. And it's not just survivors, but others who have sustained the loss of a person close to them. So many of them had the same practices for becoming and staying healthy in mind, body and spirit, but more often this wisdom came over hard time and at a significant cost. To be the graceful listener was often all they wanted, but to be a listener, who had lived in their steps, was priceless.

A PERSONAL EXPERIENCE

I attended one of the fundraising walks called "Out of Darkness" sponsored and supported by the American Foundation for Suicide Prevention (AFSP) one Saturday in late summer. I wasn't sure why I was being so mentally prodded to go during the completion of the book; I just knew I had to say yes to the experience. First of all, as a survivor I belonged among the hundreds of walkers that showed up that day. Beyond that, I simply felt that I wanted to move among people who were finding a voice for what had happened in their life. I wanted to hear their voices.

Additionally, I had been struggling with a specific chapter proposed in the book entitled "Interviews"—despite the fact I had created nine prompting questions that I hoped would uncover where survivors were succeeding or getting stuck in their recovery and healing. Somehow it wasn't coming together like I thought it would. Perhaps this event would give me some insight I seemed to be missing. I planned on using the interview questions as a starting point whenever I could.

The event had a different atmosphere than survivor self-help groups I had attended previously. There was an energy here that I couldn't name, but I was totally on alert. Surprisingly, I found myself hanging back as an observer. I didn't feel ready to move into a place of introduction and socializing. I had showed up thirty minutes ahead of registration—a dyed in the wool overachiever—and it was obvious from the onset, as people began arriving, that both the volunteers and the participants were of one mind: to make a difference. So many of them knew each other from previous years of walking; they hugged, they caught up on recent information, took photos of their teams, coffee, donuts, connecting. Many walked by me sitting alone, smiled and asked if I would join them. I became involved in conversation with two members of a large family team, representing a lovely fourteen-year-old teenager. As I talked about my own presence that day and my book, I was excitedly pulled from person to person, family member to family member, given a brief introduction, and asked to tell my book story again. Why was I writing this? What did I want to know? How could they help? On and on I was passed along because my journey seemed so important to them all. I suddenly felt part of an enormous family of like-minded people. Their loved ones had such value! The victims' representatives left on the earth were giving them such a powerful voice. I could hear those voices and felt the vibration of their presence so strongly that day, it was almost deafening. That Saturday I put aside my formal questions and listened to what they needed me to hear – not what I was asking them to say.

I spoke to one woman who was the fourteen year old teenager's aunt. This was not her first suicide survivorship. I wondered, how did she do it so many years ago as a young child when you weren't even allowed to say the word "suicide" never mind growing up with the stigma and answering all the questions that other children and people will ask?

Out of Darkness—how true this felt on that Saturday morning! I left the event with hugs, and phone numbers and requests for re-connection soon. They wanted to be part of the healing – their own and the one I was writing about. Out of Darkness— this is where we are determined to go.

The compilation of their wisdom and fearlessness, their agony and their resolve, involves phrases from survivors at every stage of post-trauma. All of it, every single sentence, has tremendous value, whether it turns on an "Aha!" in your soul or makes you weep with understanding. I know you will find yourselves there somewhere. You are ready to add your own; and well you should, since that is one more facet to confronting your emotional gauge.

By the time I drove home on the day of the survivor walk, my nine-question interview, that I thought would help to bring clarity to the long haul, had lost its function. I had over-structured the whole idea, when all I needed to do was to let the proverbial horses out of the barn, let them have their leads and not corral them. How much more revealing it became when a simple inquiry surrendered a plethora of information, not even hinted at in the formal questions! So rather than proceeding with yellow note pad and pen, I simply went forth with the general ideas stamped in my memory bank and used one or more of them to open the door to a conversation. I turned to survivors and asked for their honest responses about what helps them get up every morning, get through their day, and sleep well at night while still carrying the burden of sudden and irrefutable loss. And of course, what doesn't work. I stepped without fear into the spaces that I was sure were painful for them to explain, yet gave me another perspective outside of my own. By quietly asking, I encountered true wisdom from others. I summoned my courage and spoke to survivor after survivor about what they had learned and were continuing to learn as they traveled their recovery road.

I have listed these pearls of wisdom below, almost verbatim, "almost" because I had to remember the interaction as it occurred using nothing more than my recall and some very quick notes made immediately following each encounter. My formal interview could never have elicited the responses I was blessed to receive from these candid and honest survivors. There are other "voices" here as well, not just the statements of survivors of suicide, but survivors of other tremendous loss. We share so much in common, that the long haul is truly for us all.

* Unconditional friendship is the greatest support.
* If you are going to heal, you need to "go within" to do it.
* My loss now has the bitter edges softened by time and wonderful memories. The passing of time mellows the questions of why…
* To this day, meditation and quiet prayer, walks on the beach are the calming factors to me…
* Anger only leaves you stuck. I try not to be angry about anything anymore – it does nothing to help.
* Trying to answer the question of Why is useless. It will only hurt you more than you already are. You must find a way to leave "why" behind, or you will go crazy with grief.

❀ Let sad moments come uncensored, experience them fully, then find the positive thought and lay it right on top of the pain.

❀ Celebrating the loved one is totally healing.

❀ Not talking about the suicide of your loved one is non-healing. If you do that, then basically you can never talk about them again.

❀ Talking about your loved one is healing, and if it engages in a discussion of suicide, so be it.

❀ I know now that he was in deep pain and darkness and he could not live with that any longer. (It was his journey).

❀ Their (the victim's) journey is not my journey. I do not need to die so I can understand it, I simply need to accept it and love them anyway.

❀ Early on, the love of friends, family and our (religious advisor) kept us going.

❀ Talks with (my minister), coffee with dear friends who would not take no for an answer, helped me to keep moving forward.

❀ I do not mind if suicide comes up in conversation outside the home. I can now use the conversation in a teaching moment.

❀ By not shying away from the topic of suicide, I am giving my loved one meaning. I can also help non-survivors to understand something about a victim's conflict with himself or herself.

- I would like to share with others that for as long as you live and talk about your loved one, your loved one lives. Remember your loved one's life, not their death.
- Be there for others when you are able. It's not just about you.
- Keeping yourself and your family busy and organized may help take up the time, but it can also delay the grieving.
- I recognize that his/her journey was not mine, and the way out of this life was their choice, for whatever reason.
- Considering 7 things that have been *least helpful:*

  - Feeling guilt that I could have/should have done something.
  - Constantly thinking about Why it happened.
  - Sharing in the loss with those who are alive in drama and are living as perpetual victims of the event.
  - Giving up my freedom to make my own decisions.
  - Forgetting that I have a very powerful word at my disposal –NO
  - Believing that my life is over.
  - Not asking for help when I knew I needed it.

* I am my best support system.
* It has to start with loving ourselves, which is difficult for most of us at best.
* What I would like to share is that if your religion or person you look to for guidance tells you that God wanted another angel, or that your loved one is condemned, get away from that line of thinking quickly and ask yourself; What would a loving God, Father, Parent of all living beings, want for their children? What would you want for your loved one, when you are operating from love?
* Know that you can survive the death of a child whether by suicide, accident or a prolonged illness; it is not easy and will be with you always. But, look around you and look at our world, even with all of its weights and sorrows and madness. We are blessed to continue on and just have to know that our child is looking down on us and is proud of how we have carried on.
* I took the love shown to me during my survivorship as my shield of vulnerability, invisible, but there as an open door to my own heart. I would share this love all those who read your words, Gabrielle.
* From the moment my body conceived my child's presence, I felt the responsibility to be their

guardian for the rest of their life. I guess in my own small way I am still doing that.

* By letting go of the need to find reasons to explain their suicide to others and to myself, I let love for them and myself take its place, I declared to myself and the Universe their value and my value.

* As a human on a journey such as survivorship, we should not contribute to the stigma by being silent out of ego and fear.

* Speak out – we have something to say about suicide that can help so many others.

* This temporary gestational contract, whether accomplished in our body or someone else's body, automatically put us in a position to serve lovingly for a lifetime. That hasn't ended.

* We can spearhead appreciation for meaning in life for all survivors everywhere. We can be a part of removing the stigma.

* Being close enough to support a primary survivor (of suicide loss) is tricky business. I have my grief, but it seems tremendously reduced in comparison to his –I am the wife of his second marriage and his son was from the first one. My support of him centers around being present and observing, and then knowing when to run interference without being asked.

- The only answer to the question of Why is to stop looking for one.
- Change your thinking from "I Want" to "I Serve." If you are serving, you are giving; and if you are giving you are getting!
- Sometimes it is far easier, and therefore safer for you, to stay clear of the "big picture." Manage yourself from moment to moment, day to day and even hour by hour until gazing toward the bigger picture becomes acceptable.

CREATING NEW MEMORIES OUT OF THE OLD ONES

Back in the chapter on gratitude, I told you about celebrating Drew's birthday, nine months after he had passed. How festive it was in a joyful, sad bittersweet way, but truly celebratory just the same. Repeating that yearly didn't seem quite right for our family, although I spoke with folks that do have a birthday event each year by their own choice. As a family, we found another way to go forward by selecting a fundraiser as a pay-it-forward on or near Drew's anniversary – something the whole family could be a part of. One year it was to pass out water to walkers raising monies to pay for an eight-year-old going through chemotherapy. We see it as a "Choose not to lose. Save a life." I like that. We do it in Drew's memory and ask him to be a guardian angel to whomever the fundraiser is for. For me, it works every time to bring appreciation and honor to my son. Somehow it never brings sadness with it, but rather an opportunity to help the living. Remember the survivor's quote; you can change your thinking from "I Want" to "I Serve." When you are serving, you are giving; and if you are giving you are getting!

Like all families, our own birthdays, weddings, graduations, christenings, all have a member not physically present, but spiritually present every time, because that is where we see them and sense them. Whenever there are pictures taken in our celebrations—and probably during yours as well—lovely orbs seem to appear in the photos surrounding us. I like to believe that is our loved one being present.

SEEING THE CONNECTION TO USING
MORE THAN ONE TOOL AT A TIME

Many of the tools work in tandem with each other and cover several conditions or situations we are often faced with on a day-to-day basis. Breathing can often be overlooked especially in stressful situations - breathe better, think better. At first, use it for everything and get yourself in the habit of repeatedly slowing your pulse, lowering your blood pressure and clearing your head. Before you know it, it will happen almost automatically. Remember, everything can wait while you breathe.

When you allow, you have two possible objectives – someone else and yourself. Allowing releases the stress and pressure for both of you, no matter which direction it is going. If someone is making it challenging for you, allow that they can think what they want and it has nothing to do with you. That is *their* path. If you are making an emotional response you would like to change, allow that you are work-in-progress and it's all good. Permission granted to move on!

RECOGNIZE WHEN YOU ARE EMOTIONALLY STUCK AND THEN TAKE ACTION TO UNSTICK.

How will you know when you are getting emotionally stuck in a space that is not a positive move toward your healing? We are all different, but instinctively we know ourselves better than anyone else, right? So if you find that you are making the same decisions (or lack of decisions) in the same way as when you began your journey, and it is not helping or you are not getting the outcome you hoped for, it is time for a rethink.

* Perhaps your social interactions are permanently on hold and you have no plans for changing that

simply because isolation is easier than having to explain things like suicide. A perfect tool to engage would be *intention* – set it to give you a goal of one social interaction a week. Call a close friend, set a lunch date, go to a film or take a walk together.

* Perhaps you continue to anguish over the why of suicide. Instead of letting it consume you to find the answer, use *allowing* to move you away from that block and usher in the *releasing* of supposed guilt.

* If you are keeping your schedule so full that you simply shuffle from task to task without stopping to bring attention to your own heart's needs, change that. Using the tool of *deep breathing*, bring your nervous energies to heel. Assign time for reflection, grief, and peace and incorporate the tools of *silence and meditation*. Use the tool of *gratitude* and appreciate the time you can spend on yourself. Establish some memories that will give you a respite from sadness and substitute smile and laughter. Set an *intention* to schedule and uncover some photos or artifacts of your loved one that can soothe you and assist in memory making. *Be in the now moment* wherever you are during this time and do not think past or future.

* As you find ways to increase your opportunity to socialize, use *intention* to give yourself permission to ask others who are waiting to assist in your recovery. State clearly and honestly what it is you need, then let them help you. You learn to trust and let go and they feel loved and useful – everyone wins.

* When your brain continues to give you negative reasons and explanations for something, think a better thought. Overlay something positive onto your position, even if it's just a little. *Remember that what you think is what the Universe will give you.* So change your thinking about something, shift the thought180 degrees and see it from the other direction. Even if you can only go 90 degrees, it is far better than standing in the shadow of negativity.

By incorporating the steps in combination or by themselves, you will find that you are manifesting where you want to be emotionally and energetically.

CELEBRATE YOUR PROGRESS

When you find that you have moved away from negativity, if you see that your decision-making is feeling good to you, if you calculate a change in your heart around anger and fear, however small a step – Celebrate! Congratulate yourself on moving forward in the healing process and your body, mind and spirit will respond. You believe in yourself to find the happiness and joy you deserve; developing concrete experience in the face of tragedy is fundamental to a healthy life.

You cannot fail – there is no fail. We are all doing the very best we can with what we have and know. By allowing *yourself,* you have already given You permission to try it out and see if you can make it work. No grades, no red marks, no keeping back. Every time you are faced with a step, one that feels okay and doesn't scream "danger", say yes and take it. And when it works for you and you smile, celebrate. Do it again until it becomes exactly what your intention is. Then set another intention and watch it come to pass. You will be smiling and laughing soon enough.

AN UNEXPECTED TRIGGER

The death of comedian and actor Robin Williams this year threw my daughter and I back about 300 yards. Emma texted me just hours after Robin's suicide when the news media had made it public. She asked me, "How could another brilliant, talented person with everything they could possibly want or have at their fingertips, find no way to happiness and take their own life? What are we missing?" There I was with those very thoughts on my mind and Drew in my heart. This news, however distant from my own tragedy, still became a trigger on suicide and its place in society. How quickly I felt the fear and pull of desperation and loss, and Robin Williams was only someone I was acquainted with via movies and television. I felt I was somewhere in Robin's third ring – The Ring of Impact, where I depended on getting joy and laughter from him as an entertainer and icon, and yet, I also felt the echoes of shaky ground from flirting with the second Ring of Quake – suicide, all over again.

Here was a trigger I never saw coming down the pike. My emotional gauge was responding overtime just at the news of Robin's death. I wasn't sure how to answer my daughter's question, but I was resolved to stay with my conviction of Allowing. He just did it and thereby deprived the world of genius and deprived himself a life of joy and accomplishment. Mr. Williams made his decision without employing anyone's advice. It hurt terribly just the same.

In the long haul, the trigger will always return at intervals when you least expect it – what did we miss, what could I have done? Pulling oneself back from the declaration that "we should have known" will always be the challenge. We learn to give each person their "rights" without accepting responsibility. It's not easy, but it gets easier. And when another "episode" enters our life-book, we can use the tools to see us through the process, perhaps helping others by example. If we are professionals in the field, just maybe we are learning new ways to anticipate and help, but not fix.

A FEW WORDS ABOUT MEDIUMSHIP

The first time I encountered mediumship following Drew's death was only three weeks after he had passed. I didn't go looking for any connection here. My emotions were open and raw and the last thing I needed was to follow some expectation that my son would contact me. The only reason I went to this event was because it was a fundraiser for our town's graduation class and they needed the monies that would come from this attendance. I didn't know the medium, but was aware of her family heritage, which included tremendous credentials. I hid myself in the back of the room. During this show, the medium (whom we will call N) didn't have a mobile microphone, and anyone that she wished to interact with in the audience had to go up on stage so that the mic would pick up their voices. Halfway through, N looked out into the audience and straight into my eyes and said, "There are mothers here that have lost children." Two women raised their hands – I stayed mute. N walked further out into the audience, as far as her cord would allow and stood looking at me. I shrank. "I feel the loss of a child – recently." My friend who had begged me to come to this event with her, literally pointed to me. Before I knew it, I was standing on this stage. I was absolutely, inequitably paralyzed. Now I must tell you that I have been doing stage work in the public since a very young age, often in groups as large as 300 people, stage productions, lectures, trainings….I am fearless in big crowds and audiences. At this moment I couldn't move! There were less than fifty people in front of me and I was nearly faint with fear. Why? Because my son was one of the most private humans on the planet and this young woman in front of me was about to bring my private hell to the public.

She rattled off names of people in my family; she described professions that my family members engaged in, she quoted cards that were received and the exact words that were written in them – all things she could never have known. I had never seen her before in my life. Then she looked at me and whispered, "Your son will not say anything in front of these people; he will not talk about his passing or any circumstances surrounding it, but he wants you to have a private session, because he has much to say to you. Here is my card; I will do this private reading at no cost. Please, call me!" I eventually did, but the important point is that, without realizing I was doing it, I utilized several tools, namely deep breathing and allowing. This is what got me through the experience that evening. I eventually chose the date and time, when I was in control of my emotional readiness. That, however, is another story.

The moral here is...

Rule #1: Don't let anyone talk you into a mediumship experience if you don't want one or aren't prepared to go to one. This sort of exposure is a calling for the medium and a curiosity for the rest of us, but it is a *very* personal decision for you. Allow that much of the world is fascinated by the unknown, and allow that your choice to participate in this should be purely your decision. The day may come that you wish to explore the metaphysical in relationship to departed loved ones, but not at the cost of your wellbeing. I literally thought I was about to join my son in death in the few moments I was on that stage and it was not worth the terror.

Rule #2: Don't go before you are ready if you are drawn to it. You will know if and when that time comes, but not sooner than you are emotionally prepared for what takes place. Or doesn't take place. Meditating and being in the now moment may help you with answers to your questions. At a reading, the disappointment can be huge if your expectations are set high and then nothing happens. This is such a personal decision that I can't say enough about it. Do remember the tool of manifesting what you think. If you are a total non-believer about the possibility of being contacted by a loved one, why in the world would you pay good money for the experience?

Rule #3: My final point to this topic and actually any request toward you and your healing business, is to say NO or YES, but be in the moment and do what your heart is telling you to do – be still and figure it out. Feel your emotional gauges and what they register. You will make the right decisions by listening to them and not other people. What do you need right now? How does this feel right this moment? My answer to all things rests with the very second I am in this experience, and I will know what to do. I am free to make a choice based on what I intuitively feel right now and no one on the outside of me should push me into a decision.

HINTS FOR COMBINING THE STEPS
TO WORK WITH EACH OTHER

Deep breathing is the one tool that is universally paired with every other tool in your backpack. It works when you are under fire or stress, and it works when you need a break from just coping. Deep breathing is your body balancer at all times and in all scenarios.

Combining the tools of *Intention, Deep Breathing* and *Allowing*

- Almost every allowing opportunity is easily combined with an intention.
- Once you recognize that you need to allow in any way, you can form the intention statement and use it whenever the situation arises of "fixing" what doesn't belong to you.
- Through intention, you can open a path to your goal, whatever that may be.
- Others may tell or insinuate that you could have intervened and perhaps prevented a disastrous outcome. You can set an intention surrounding eliminating self-blame.
- The intention: There is only my truth. I am guilt-free.
- You allow them to have their thoughts about intervention-in-the-nick-of-time philosophies. It has nothing to do with you or your thoughts.
- Deep breathing will give you the interval and relaxation to manage these conversations better.
- Anger and blame is a temporary response that can turn into a permanent way of life. We must allow others to make their own way through the pain, but we do not have to embrace their beliefs.

* Say to yourself, "I am allowing you to have your thoughts and opinions about this tragedy. They are not my thoughts and I will not believe any false statements that come from them."

Combining the tools of *Deep Breathing* and *Being in the Now Moment*

* You are feeling fragile and overwhelmed with what is ahead.
* Find your feet and be in the now moment, actively recognizing the emotions, beauty, situation, environment you are in at this very time.
* Take a balancing and *deep breath*. What do you want and feel *now*, and accept it. All is well with whatever decisions are required. Make your decisions with confidence.

Combining the tools of *Gratitude/Appreciation, Deep Breathing and Being in the Now Moment*

* You feel sad and jealous at someone else's happiness. *Deep breathe* through your anger and resentment.
* You can be *grateful* for your own memories, and *appreciate* that someone else is making some of their own.

* Take in the *now moment* and feel healing in these positive thoughts.
* When you are *in the now moment* and you find joy in what you are experiencing exactly where your feet are, then *gratitude and appreciation* for that joy should be acknowledged.
* To be in the *now moment* almost always puts you in a position to *deep breathe* and balance the body system.

Combining *Gratitude/Appreciation and Abundance* with *You Manifest What You Think or law of attraction.*

* You can envision your success through positive thought and a healing goal using *law of attraction*, then experience the joy when it comes to fruition, otherwise known as *abundance. Gratitude* is one way to say Thank You to you.
* If you are able to bring yourself 180 degrees around to seeing the positive side of any situation, even if it is a small change, and it brings you relief, then *appreciation* is a tool to engage.

Perhaps one of the most obvious tool combinations can be *Silence/Meditation and Release* with *Deep Breathing* and *Allowing*

* It is through and with *deep breathing* that we are able to place ourselves in a state of calm relaxation sufficient to go within.

* When you are *meditating or silent* within, you are aware of healing. For this simple act, you can be *grateful.*

* It is a perfect time to *release* any concerns you may have for what has not been done and what lies ahead.

* When we *allow* ourselves or we *allow* for others, we provide us with an opportunity to *release* the need to coerce, compromise, defend and agree, knowing it is in our best interest.

There are a number of tools that work co-operatively with *manifesting what you think*

* When you decide that your positive approach to word usage is to be part of your healing, engage *intention-setting* as its partner.

* *Allow* that the learning curve for you is acceptable however you use it and you will feel *gratitude and appreciation* for your success even if it seems slow at the beginning.

* Be in the *now moment* and *mindful* whenever you are using language that will directly reflect your

current emotional status, for you are in control of how good it can make you feel.

Some final thoughts

Whenever I needed guidance in the writing of this book, and asked for it, it always came; even in the middle of the night, with a small pad and a lighted pen! Somehow I knew that if I didn't capture those incredible thoughts right then, they would be gone in the morning no matter how much I promised myself that I would remember. What I was driven by passion to say to the millions of people who have lost their loved ones to suicide was far too important to leave to chance or to a sleepy memory. Most importantly, *you don't have to find a reason to get up each day. You ARE the reason.* Life is so precious. By embracing all the beauty and vibrancies that our planet has to offer, we show our love and appreciation for it and for ourselves. Be grateful for the opportunity, be surprised each time your thoughts manifest something you have wished for, totally engage the very moment you belly laugh because that is now, not tomorrow, not yesterday. Rejoice when you refrain from solving a problem that doesn't belong to you, and when you find relief from not absorbing someone else's opinion. Appreciate yourself. Celebrate yourself! Be still and hear your own sweet voice say to you, "I am loved, I am at peace, I don't need anything".

Acknowledgments

To Angelo, for putting up with the bright blue lighted pen hovering over the notepad in the middle of the night.

To Lisa, my BEFF. (She knows what that means).

To the dear ones who read for me; Carol, Sue G, Marianne, Susan R and Karen. It seems I owe you guys some boxes of tissues.

And Chris.

Resources and
References

"An investment in knowledge
pays the best interest."

— BENJAMIN FRANKLIN

REFERENCES
1-Diaphragmatic breathing: Wikipedia Free Encyclopedia
http://en.wikipedia.org/wiki/Diaphragmatic_
breathing
2 - *National Center for Complementary and Alternative
Medicine (NCCAM)*
https://nccih.nih.gov/health/stress/relaxation.htm

3 - To learn more about exposure therapy:
http://psychcentral.com/lib/what-is-exposure-therapy/
0001640

To learn more about meditation:
well.blogs.nytimes.com/2011/01/28/how-meditation-may-change-the-brain
How Meditation May Change the Brain (January 28, 2011) By Sindya N. Bhanoo

RESOURCES

1) NIMH – National Institute of Mental Health
2) AFSP - American Foundation for Suicide Prevention
3) AAS - American Association of Suicidology
4) WHO - World Health Organization
5) CDC - Center for Disease Control

RESEARCH NOTES
Researchers report that those who meditated for about 30 minutes a day for eight weeks had measurable changes in gray-matter density in parts of the

brain associated with memory, sense of self, empathy and stress. The findings can be found in <u>Psychiatry Research: Neuroimaging.</u>

M.R.I. brain scans taken before and after the participants' meditation regimen found increased gray matter in the hippocampus, an area important for learning and memory. The images also showed a reduction of gray matter in the amygdala, a region connected to anxiety and stress. A control group that did not practice meditation showed no such changes.

Britta Hölzel, a psychologist at Massachusetts General Hospital and Harvard Medical School and the study's lead author, said the participants practiced mindfulness meditation, a form of meditation that was introduced in the United States in the late 1970s. It traces its roots to the same ancient Buddhist techniques.

<u>Am J Psychiatry.</u> 2003 Aug;160(8):1525-6.

FAMILY HISTORY OF SUICIDE
AMONG SUICIDE VICTIMS
Runeson B[1], Asberg M.
Author information: Karoliniska Institute, Department of Clinical Neuroscience, Section for Psychiatry, St.

Goran's Hospital, Stockholm, Sweden. bo.runeson@
spo.sll.se

ABSTRACT

Objective: The aim was to compare the rates of suicide
in family members of suicide victims and comparison
subjects who died of other causes.

Method: The Swedish cause of death register identified all suicides in subjects born between 1949 and 1969
(N=8,396). The comparison group comprised persons
of the same age who died of other causes (N=7,568).
First-degree relatives of the suicide victims (N=33,173)
and comparison subjects (N=28,945) were identified.

Results: Among families of the suicide victims there
were 287 suicides, representing 9.4% of all deaths in family members. Among comparison families there were 120
suicides, 4.6% of all deaths. The difference was significant. Previous psychiatric care and suicide in a family
member predicted suicide in the logistic regression
model.

Conclusions: The rate of suicide was twice as high in
families of suicide victims as in comparison families. A
family history of suicide predicted suicide independent
of severe mental disorder

AGENCIES

LIFE INSURANCE

http://www.insurancequotes.org/life/the-truth-about-suicide-life-insurance/

http://thereinhangsatale.blogspot.com/2012/09/understand-suicide-clause-in-life.html

GROUPS AND WEBSITES FOR SURVIVORS

http://www.afsp.org/coping-with-suicide/find-support/find-a-support-group

http://www.afsp.org/coping-with-suicide/find-support/survivor-outreach-program

http://www.afsp.org/coping-with-suicide/international-survivors-of-suicide-loss-day

http://samaritansnyc.org/surviving-a-suicide-loss/

MATERIALS

http://tinybuddha.com/blog/5-lessons-about-being-present-freedom-is-where-my-feet-are/

http://www.amazon.com/s/?ie=UTF8&keywords=mindful+meditation/

http://www.guidedimagerydownloads.com/

http://www.lionsroar.com/mindful-living-thich-nhat-hanh-on-the-practice-of-mindfulness-march-2010/
http://www.law-of-attraction-guide.com/history-of-the-law-of-attraction.html
http://www.cmhc.utexas.edu/stressrecess/Level_Two/breathing.html

MILITARY

http://www.stripes.com/news/military-suicide-survivors-help-each-other-heal-at-seminar-1.310858

The National Military Suicide Survivor Seminar recently convened in St. Petersburg, Fla. The program is organized by the Tragedy Assistance Program for Survivors (TAPS), a non-profit group that provides assistance to loved ones of fallen troops. This year's event drew roughly 650 survivors from around the country, all of whom lost a service member to suicide.

BOOKS

Esther and Jerry Hicks, *The Law of Attraction*
Barbara Rubel, *But I Didn't Say Goodbye: Helping Children and Families After a Suicide*
Jeffrey Jackson, *SOS Handbook*
Christopher Lucas, *Living in the Wake of Suicide*

Dr. Masaru Emoto, *The Hidden Messages in Water,*
Pam Grout, *E2*
Dr. Wayne Dyer, *Wishes Fulfilled*

CD's

1. The Ribbon Breath
   www.meditationhealing.com/the-ribbon-breath-meditation-s/1818.htm
2. The Healing Waterfall – Max Highstein
3. The Healing Waterfall III – Max Highstein
4. Marianne Williamson – Meditations for a Miraculous Life
   (This CD is based on a series of prayers that are delivered as guided imagery)

BLOGS

http://survivorhealing.com/blog (by Gabrielle Doucet)
campkita.com/blog
allianceofhope.org/blog
http://www.pocketmindfulness.com/6-mindfulness-exercises-you-can-try-today/ (by Alfred James)

About the Author

Gabrielle Doucet is a registered nurse, healing energy practitioner, and author. As a person of spirit, she's spent the last eleven years helping people improve their health, reduce stress through gaining awareness of the mind-body connection, and achieve a more balanced lifestyle through education and adjustment of landscape and environment.

She developed a program for people to experience personal healing from pain, injury, fear, anxiety, sadness, and chronic and acute illness. This program works by putting people in control and giving them tools to cope, minute by minute, on their own.

Doucet holds a BSN, an MBA, and an MHA. She designs healing and stress-free gardens and landscapes for cancer patients, cancer survivors, and local garden sites, and she also provides free healing clinics for clients in need. She lives in the northeastern United States.

To Contact Gabrielle Doucet:

gabrielle@survivorhealing.com

39700701R00158

Made in the USA
San Bernardino, CA
01 October 2016